GRADE 3
Units

3 | 4

Student Edition Units 3-400

Certified by Illustrative Mathematics®

ISBN 978-1-7924-6351-8

K5_v1

20211204

Unit 3: Wrapping Up Addition and Subtraction Within 1,000...... 5

Section A: Add Within 1,000

Lesson 1: Represent Numbers in Different Ways 7

Lesson 2: Addition and Subtraction Situations 10

Lesson 3: Add Your Way 14

Lesson 4: Introduction to Addition Algorithms 17

Lesson 5: Another Addition Algorithm 21

Lesson 6: Use Strategies and Algorithms to Add............... 25

Section A Practice Problems 31

Section B: Subtract Within 1,000

Lesson 7: Subtract Your Way 38

Lesson 8: Subtraction Algorithms (Part 1)..................... 42

Lesson 9: Subtraction Algorithms (Part 2)..................... 45

Lesson 10: Subtraction Algorithms (Part 3) 49

Lesson 11: Analyze Subtraction Algorithms 52

Lesson 12: Subtract Strategically 55

Section B Practice Problems 61

Section C: Round Within 1,000

Lesson 13: Multiples of 100................................... 66

Lesson 14: Nearest Multiples of 10 and 100 70

Lesson 15: Round to the Nearest Ten and Hundred............. 74

Lesson 16: Round and Round Again 77

Section C Practice Problems 80

Section D: Solve Two-Step Problems

Lesson 17: Does It Make Sense?. 82

Lesson 18: Diagrams and Equations for Word Problems. 85

Lesson 19: Situations and Equations. 88

Lesson 20: More Practice to Represent and Solve 91

Lesson 21: Classroom Supplies 95

Section D Practice Problems. 99

Unit 4: Relating Multiplication to Division 103

Section A: What is Division?

Lesson 1: How Many Groups?. 105

Lesson 2: How Many in Each Group?. 108

Lesson 3: Division Situation Drawings. 112

Lesson 4: Interpret Division Expressions 116

Lesson 5: Write Division Expressions 120

Section A Practice Problems. 124

Section B: Relate Multiplication and Division

Lesson 6: Division as an Unknown Factor. 130

Lesson 7: Relate Multiplication and Division 133

Lesson 8: Relate Quotients to Familiar Products. 136

Lesson 9: Patterns in the Multiplication Table. 139

Lesson 10: Explore Multiplication Strategies with Rectangles. . . . 142

Lesson 11: Multiplication Strategies on Ungridded Rectangles . . 145

Section B Practice Problems. 149

Section C: Multiplying Larger Numbers

Lesson 12: Multiply Multiples of Ten 152

Lesson 13: Solve Problems With Equal Groups 156

Lesson 14: Ways to Represent Multiplication of Teen Numbers. . 159

Lesson 15: Equal Groups, Larger Numbers 162

Lesson 16: Multiply Numbers Larger than 20 165

Lesson 17: Use the Four Operations to Solve Problems 171

Section C Practice Problems 175

Section D: Dividing Larger Numbers

Lesson 18: Larger Numbers in Equal Groups. 180

Lesson 19: Ways to Divide Larger Numbers. 183

Lesson 20: Strategies for Dividing 187

Lesson 21: Solve Problems Using the Four Operations 191

Lesson 22: School Community Garden 195

Section D Practice Problems. 199

Glossary 202

Attributions 205

Citations 208

GRADE 3
Unit

3

Student Edition Units 3-4

Certified by Illustrative Mathematics®

Section A: Add Within 1,000

Lesson 1: Represent Numbers in Different Ways

- Let's represent numbers in different ways.

Warm-up: Which One Doesn't Belong: Numbers within 1,000

Which one doesn't belong?

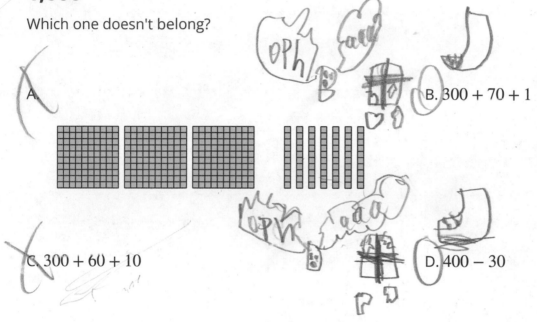

A.

B. $300 + 70 + 1$

C. $300 + 60 + 10$

D. $400 - 30$

1.1: Card Sort: Numbers in Their Different Forms

Your teacher will give you a set of cards that show numbers in different forms.

Match the cards that represent the same number. Record your matches here. Be ready to explain your reasoning.

Card Sort: Numbers in Their Different Forms A 175	Card Sort: Numbers in Their Different Forms E three hundred twenty-nine	Card Sort: Numbers in Their Different Forms I 299
Card Sort: Numbers in Their Different Forms B $800 + 10 + 3$	Card Sort: Numbers in Their Different Forms F 371	Card Sort: Numbers in Their Different Forms J
Card Sort: Numbers in Their Different Forms C 	Card Sort: Numbers in Their Different Forms G one hundred seventy-five	Card Sort: Numbers in Their Different Forms K 329
Card Sort: Numbers in Their Different Forms D two hundred ninety-nine	Card Sort: Numbers in Their Different Forms H 813	Card Sort: Numbers in Their Different Forms L $100 + 60 + 15$

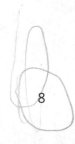

iM KH

1.2: Numbers in Different Forms Round Table

Your teacher will give you a recording sheet.

Part 1

1. In Box 1, write a three-digit number. (Pause for your teacher's instructions.)

2. In Box 2, show a way that the number could be decomposed. (Pause for teacher instructions.)

3. In Box 3, show a way that the number could be decomposed that's different from Box 2. (Pause for teacher instructions.)

4. In Box 4, show a way that the number could be decomposed that's different from Boxes 2 and 3.

Part 2

1. Look at the different ways your number was decomposed on your recording sheet. What connections do you see between them?

2. Look at all of the recording sheets for your group. What patterns do you notice in the ways the numbers are decomposed?

Lesson 2: Addition and Subtraction Situations

• Let's solve problems involving addition and subtraction.

Warm-up: Notice and Wonder: Two Curious Tables

What do you notice? What do you wonder?

+	10	20	30	40	50
10	20	30	40	50	60
20	30	40	50	60	70
30	40	50	6?	70	80
40	50	60	70	80	90
50	60	70	80	90	100

+	10	20	30	40	50
10	20	30	40	50	60
20	30	40	50	60	70
30	40	50	6?	70	80
40	50	60	70	80	90
50	60	70	80	90	100

2.1: Monuments and Falls

Solve each problem. Explain or show your reasoning.

1. Iguazu Falls in South America marks the border between Paraguay, Brazil, and Argentina. It is the largest waterfall in the world.

   The waterfall has two parts. The water falls 115 feet in the first part and 131 feet in the second part. How far down does the water fall altogether?

246

2. In Washington, D.C., there are many monuments that honor important people in American history.

   The Lincoln Memorial is 99 feet tall. The Washington Monument is 555 feet tall.

How much taller is the Washington Monument than the Lincoln Memorial?

456

349=10

3. The Eiffel Tower in Paris, France, has 674 steps that go from the ground to the second floor. There are 328 steps from the ground to the first floor.

How many steps are there from the first floor to the second floor?

$674 - 328 = 346$

346

iM KH

2.2: Journal About Connections

Respond to one of these journal prompts:

- What math did you do today that connected to something you did in an earlier grade?

- Describe something you really understand after today's lesson.

- Describe something that was confusing, challenging, or that you'd like to learn more about.

_____

_____

_____

_____

Lesson 3: Add Your Way

- Let's add numbers within 1,000.

Warm-up: Number Talk: Hundreds, Tens, and Ones

Find the value of each expression mentally.

- $200 + 40 + 7$

- $50 + 300 + 2$

- $40 + 600 + 12$

- $500 + 17 + 130$

iM KH

3.1: Strategies to Add

Find the value of each sum in any way that makes sense to you. Explain or show your reasoning.

1. $325 + 102 = 427$

$300 + 20 + 5$
$100 + 00 + 2$

325
$+ 102$
$\overline{427}$

$400 + 20 + 7 = 427$

2. $301 + 52 = 353$

3. $276 + 118 = 394$

$200 + 20 + 6$
$100 + 10 + 8$
$\overline{300 + 80 + 14 = 394}$

276
$+ 118$
$\overline{394}$

4. $298 + 305 = 603$

$300 + 00 + 1$
$00 + 50 + 2$
$\overline{300 + 50 + 3 \quad 53}$

301
$+ 52$
$\overline{353}$

$200 + 90 + 8$
$300 + 00 + 5$
$\overline{500 + 90 + 13 = 603}$

298
$+ 305$
$\overline{603}$

3.2: Two Ways to Add

Andre found the value of $276 + 118$. His work is shown.

$$200 + 100 = 300$$
$$70 + 10 = 80$$
$$6 + 8 = 14$$
$$300 + 80 + 14 = 394$$

Clare found the value of $276 + 118$. Her work is shown.

$$6 + 8 = 14$$
$$70 + 10 = 80$$
$$200 + 100 = 300$$
$$14 + 80 + 300 = 394$$

With your partner, discuss:

- What's different about Clare and Andre's work?

- What's the same?

iM KH

Lesson 4: Introduction to Addition Algorithms

- Let's learn new ways to add.

Warm-up: Which One Doesn't Belong: 247

Which one doesn't belong?

A. $200 + 30 + 17$

B. 247

C. $200 + 47 + 10$

D. $100 + 140 + 7$

4.1: What is an Algorithm?

Three students found the value of 362 + 354. Their work is shown. Explain how each method works.

1. Tyler's drawing

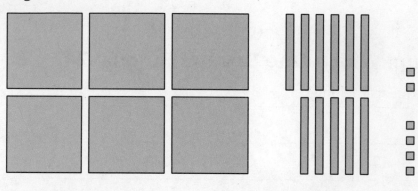

_____

_____

_____

2. Lin's method

$$
\begin{array}{r}
300 + 60 + 2 \\
+ \quad 300 + 50 + 4 \\
\hline
600 + 110 + 6
\end{array}
$$

_____

_____

_____

3. Han's method

```
    3 6 2
  + 3 5 4
  ───────
        6
    1 1 0
  + 6 0 0
  ───────
    7 1 6
```

_____

_____

_____

_____

4.2: Try an Algorithm

Try using an algorithm to find the value of each sum. Show your thinking. Organize it so it can be followed by others.

1. $475 + 231$

2. $136 + 389$

3. $670 + 257$

Lesson 5: Another Addition Algorithm

- Let's learn another algorithm to add.

Warm-up: Notice and Wonder: Another Curious Table

What do you notice? What do you wonder?

+	98	99	100	101	102
98	99	197	198	199	200
99	197	198	199	200	201
100	98	199	200	201	202
101	199	200	201	202	203
102	200	201	202	203	204

5.1: A New Addition Algorithm

Here are two algorithms for adding $367 + 231$.

Han's algorithm

Hans

```
    3  6  7
 +  2  3  1
          8     step 1
       9  0     step 2
 +  5  0  0     step 3
    5  9  8     step 4
```

uses place value

Elena's algorithm

```
    3  6  7              3  6  7              3  6  7
 +  2  3  1           +  2  3  1           +  2  3  1
          8   step 1        9  8   step 2     5  9  8   step 3
```

Discuss with your partner:

1. How is Elena's algorithm different from Han's algorithm?

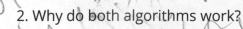

Elena make more the nice way

2. Why do both algorithms work?

we did hers we do.

iM KH

5.2: Compose New Units

Here are two algorithms for adding $365 + 182$.

Han's algorithm

```
    3  6  5
 +  1  8  2
 ───────────
          7    step 1
    1  4  0    step 2
 +  4  0  0    step 3
 ───────────
    5  4  7    step 4
```

Elena's algorithm

```
                 1  0  0            1  0  0
    3  6  5       3  6  5            3  6  5
 +  1  8  2    +  1  8  2         +  1  8  2
 ──────────    ──────────         ──────────
          7          4  7             5  4  7
   step 1          step 2             step 3
```

1. How do the algorithms show the 14 tens differently?

$= 140$

$14 \times 10 = 140$

2. Try Elena's algorithm to find the value of each sum.

   a. $174 + 352$

b. 273 + 619

c. 354 + 198

d. 525 + 376

Lesson 6: Use Strategies and Algorithms to Add

- Let's consider when to use algorithms and when to use other strategies to add.

Warm-up: Number Talk: Little More, Little Less

Find the value of each expression mentally.

- $300 + 156 = 456$

- $299 + 156 = 455$

- $303 + 156 = 459$

- $204 + 376 = 580$

6.1: Just Ones

Two methods of recording the addition of 657 + 286 are shown.

Method 1

```
      1  0  0
         1  0
      6  5  7
   +  2  8  6
   ─────────
      9  4  3
```

Method 2

```
      1  1
      6  5  7
   +  2  8  6
   ──────────
      9  4  3
```

1. How is the newly composed ten and hundred recorded differently in each method?

2. Try the second method of recording to add these numbers:

    a. 602 + 179

    b. 493 + 161

26

c. 438 + 364

d. 329 + 381

6.2: How Would You Add?

Use a strategy of your choice to find the value of each sum. Show your reasoning.
Organize it so it can be followed by others.

1. $199 + 348$

2. $264 + 359$

3. $203 + 75$

4. 316 + 198

5. 399 + 499 $= 898$

$+\begin{array}{r}399\\499\\\hline 898\end{array}$

$99 + 99 = 198$

$300 + 400 = 700$

$700 + 198 = 898$

Section A Summary

In this section, we learned that an **algorithm** is a set of steps that works every time as long as the steps are carried out correctly. Then, we learned algorithms to add numbers within 1,000.

We also learned that we can choose to add using a strategy or an algorithm based on the numbers being added.

```
    300 +  60 +  2              3 6 2              1 0 0              1  1.
  +  300 +  50 +  9          +  3 5 9            1 0            3 6 2            3 6 2
    600 + 110 + 11                1 1          3 6 2          + 3 5 9          + 3 5 9
                               1 1 0          + 3 5 9          7 2 1          7 2 1
                             +  6 0 0          7 2 1
                                7 2 1
```

iM KH

Section A Practice Problems

1. Pre-unit

Which number could be labeled on the number line?

A. 23

B. 45

C. 77

D. 92

2. Pre-unit

There are 85 students on the playground. There are 57 fewer students in the classroom than on the playground. How many students are in the classroom? Explain or show your reasoning.

3. Pre-unit

Jada says she can find $87 - 59$ by taking away 60 from 87 and adding 1 so it is the same as $27 + 1$ or 28. Explain or show why Jada's method to calculate $87 - 59$ makes sense.

4. Pre-unit

10+20+800≈830

Find the value of 316 + 514. Explain or show your reasoning.

830   6+4=10

300+500=800

5. Pre-unit   10+10=20

Put a < or > in the blank to make each statement true.

a. 197 __<__ 311

b. 567 __≥__ 555

c. 908 __>__ 809

6. Pre-unit

Find the value of each expression.

a. 206 + 543 =744

b. 327 + 181 =508

c. 674 − 129 =545

iM KH

7. Select all representations of the number four hundred twenty-three.

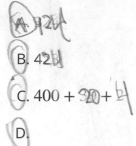

A. 924

B. 423

C. 400 + 20 + 3

D.

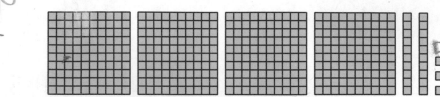

E.

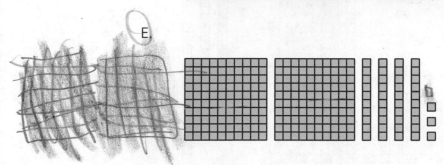

(From Unit 3, Lesson 1.)

8. The height of the Empire State Building in New York City is 443 meters. The tallest building in the world is 820 meters. How many meters taller than the Empire State Building is the tallest building in the world?

2 - 121

(From Unit 3, Lesson 2.)

9. Find the value of each sum in any way that makes sense to you. Explain or show your reasoning.

a. 456 + 231

b. $372 + 165$

(From Unit 3, Lesson 3.)

10. Here are three different ways to find the value of $157 + 436$.

A

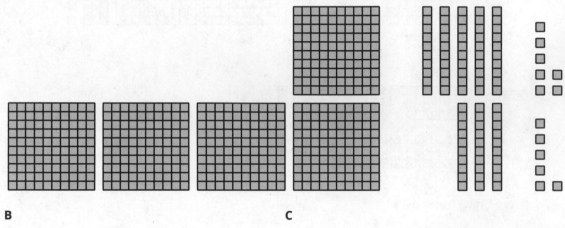

B

$$
\begin{array}{r}
100 + 50 + 7 \\
+ \quad 400 + 30 + 6 \\
\hline
500 + 80 + 13
\end{array}
$$

C

$$
\begin{array}{r}
1\ 5\ 7 \\
+\ 4\ 3\ 6 \\
\hline
1\ 3 \\
8\ 0 \\
5\ 0\ 0 \\
\hline
5\ 9\ 3
\end{array}
$$

How are the methods alike? How are they different? Explain your reasoning.

_____

_____

_____

_____

(From Unit 3, Lesson 4.)

iM KH

11. Here is Elena's algorithm for finding $273 + 481$.

```
                   1 0 0              1 0 0
    2 7 3          2 7 3              2 7 3
  + 4 8 1        + 4 8 1            + 4 8 1
  ---------      ---------          ---------
        4  step 1     5 4  step 2     7 5 4  step 3
```

a. Where does the 100 that Elena wrote in step 2 come from?

b. Use Elena's method to find $255 + 372$.

(From Unit 3, Lesson 5.)

12. a. What do the 1s above the 2 and 5 in 253 mean in this calculation?

```
    1 1
    2 5 3
  +   8 9
  ---------
    3 4 2
```

b. Use an algorithm or another strategy to find the value of each sum.

     i. $572 + 268$

     ii. $726 + 199$

(From Unit 3, Lesson 6.)

13. **Exploration**

Here is Lin's strategy to find the value of $596 + 385$: "I added 600 and then took away 4."

    a. Explain why Lin's strategy works. Then, use it to find the value of $596 + 385$.

iM KH

b. For which of these expressions would you use Lin's strategy? Explain or show your reasoning.

   i. $436 + 173$

   ii. $517 + 255$

   iii. $787 + 135$

   iv. $247 + 395$

14. **Exploration**

   Write an addition problem with 3-digit numbers that you think is well suited for each of the following methods. Then, find the value of the sum using that method.

   a. mental strategies

   b. base-ten blocks

   c. an algorithm

Section B: Subtract Within 1,000

Lesson 7: Subtract Your Way

- Let's subtract numbers within 1,000.

Warm-up: Number Talk: Subtract Two-Digit Numbers

Find the value of each expression mentally.

- 50 – 10 = 40

- 58 – 10 = 48

- 258 – 20 = 238

- 258 – 24 = 234

iM KH

7.1: Strategies to Subtract

Find the value of each difference in any way that makes sense to you. Explain or show your reasoning.

1. 428 – 213 $= 215$

$$428$$
$$- 213$$
$$\overline{}$$
$$215$$

2. 505 – 398 $= 103$

3. 394 – 127 $= 267$

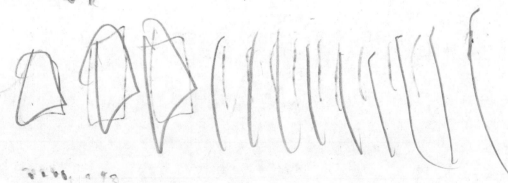

$300 + 90 + 4 = 394 - 127 = 267$

10 $0f$ $20 + 7 = 127$

7.2: Base-ten Drawings

1. Jada and Han made drawings to show how they used base-ten blocks to find the value of 262 − 135. Their drawings are shown.

Jada's drawing

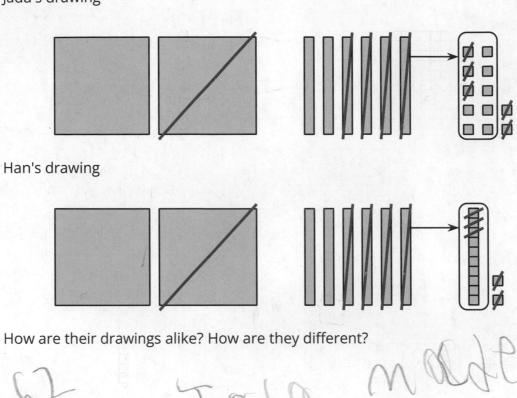

Han's drawing

How are their drawings alike? How are they different?

262
−135
127

Jada made 12 ones both Reagrewp with base ten

bloks

Hons made 10+2 ones

2. Here are three expressions, followed by three diagrams. Write each expression next to the diagram that represents it. Then, find the value of the expression.

$252 - 181 = 71$ $262 - 135 = 127$ $252 - 132 = 120$

a.

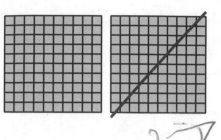 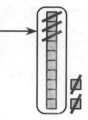

127

$$\begin{array}{r} 262 \\ -135 \\ \hline 127 \end{array}$$

b.

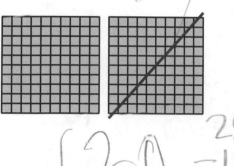

120

$$\begin{array}{r} 252 \\ -132 \\ \hline 120 \end{array}$$

c.

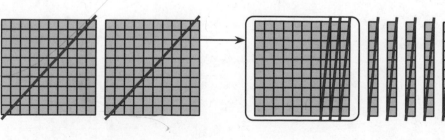

71

$$\begin{array}{r} 252 \\ -181 \\ \hline 71 \end{array}$$

Lesson 8: Subtraction Algorithms (Part 1)

- Let's learn a new way to subtract.

Warm-up: Number Talk: Subtraction Strategies

Find the value of each expression mentally.

- $100 - 98$ $= 2$ ☺

- $101 - 99$ $= 2$ ☺

- $200 - 98$ $= 102$ ☺

- $204 - 98$ $= 106$ ☺

iM KH

8.1: From Drawings to an Algorithm

Jada and Kiran found the value of $391 - 215$. Their work is shown.

Jada's drawing

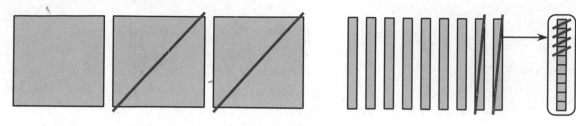

Kiran's algorithm

$$
\begin{array}{r}
\overset{80}{}\ \ \overset{11}{} \\
300 + \cancel{90} + \cancel{1} \\
-\ \ 200 + 10 + 5 \\
\end{array}
$$

$$
\begin{array}{r}
391 \\
-\ 215 \\
\hline
186 \\
\end{array}
$$

1. Explain how Kiran's algorithm starts.

   _____

   _____

2. Explain how Kiran recorded the decomposition of the ten into more ones.

   _____

   _____

3. Finish Kiran's work.

8.2: Card Sort: Diagrams and Algorithms

Your teacher will give you a set of cards. Match each diagram with an algorithm.

A

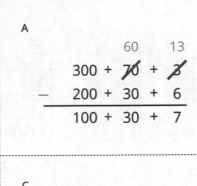

$$\begin{array}{r} 60 \quad 13 \\ 300 + \cancel{70} + \cancel{3} \\ - \quad 200 + 30 + 6 \\ \hline 100 + 30 + 7 \end{array}$$

B

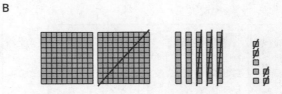

C

$$\begin{array}{r} 200 + 50 + 7 \\ - \quad 100 + 30 + 4 \\ \hline 100 + 20 + 3 \end{array}$$

D

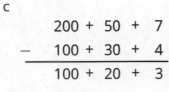

E

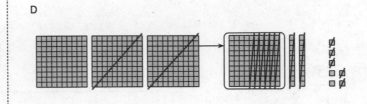

F

$$\begin{array}{r} 200 \quad 120 \\ \cancel{300} + \cancel{20} + 7 \\ - \quad 100 + 80 + 5 \\ \hline 100 + 40 + 2 \end{array}$$

G

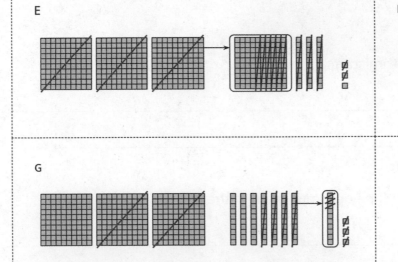

H

$$\begin{array}{r} 200 \quad 130 \\ \cancel{300} + \cancel{30} + 3 \\ - \quad 200 + 90 + 2 \\ \hline 0 + 40 + 1 \end{array}$$

iM KH

Lesson 9: Subtraction Algorithms (Part 2)

- Let's learn more about our first subtraction algorithm.

Warm-up: True or False: Does It Commute?

Decide if each statement is true or false. Be prepared to explain your reasoning.

- $4 \times 5 = 5 \times 4$

- $125 + 200 = 200 + 125$

- $300 - 100 = 100 - 300$

9.1: Revise Subtraction Work

Lin's work for finding the value of $428 - 156$ is shown.

$$
\begin{array}{r}
400 + 20 + 8 \\
-\quad 100 + 50 + 6 \\
\hline
300 + 30 + 2
\end{array}
$$

1. What error do you see in Lin's work?

2. What would you tell or show Lin so she can revise her work?

9.2: Try the Algorithm

Here is a subtraction algorithm you saw in an earlier lesson:

$$
\begin{array}{r}
 80 11 \\
300 + \cancel{90} + \cancel{1} \\
-\ \ 200 + 10 + 5 \\
\hline
\end{array}
$$

Try using this algorithm to find the value of each difference. Show your reasoning. Organize it so it can be followed by others.

1. $283 - 159$

2. $425 - 192$

3. $639 - 465$

4. 591 − 128

5. 832 − 575

iM KH

Lesson 10: Subtraction Algorithms (Part 3)

- Let's learn another algorithm to subtract.

Warm-up: Notice and Wonder: Digits that Disappear

What do you notice? What do you wonder?

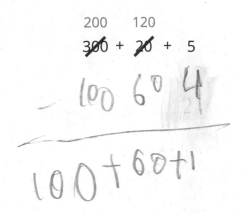

$$200 \quad 120$$
$$\cancel{300} + \cancel{20} + 5$$
$$- \quad 100 \quad 6^0{}_2 \quad 4$$
$$\overline{100 + 60 + 1}$$

$$2 \quad 12$$
$$\cancel{3}\,\cancel{2}\,5$$
$$- \quad 1 \; 6^4$$
$$\overline{1 \; 6 \; 1}$$

10.1: A New Subtraction Algorithm

Andre and Clare found the value of $528 - 271$. How they started their work is shown.

Andre's algorithm

Clare's algorithm

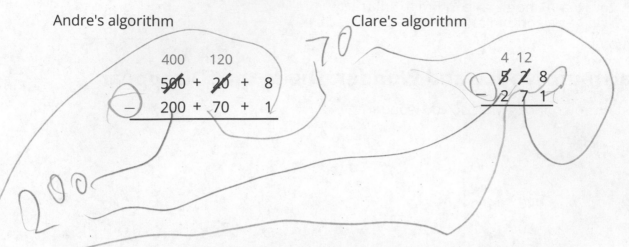

1. Complete both algorithms to find the difference.

2. Andre and Clare started their subtraction in different ways. How did their way of starting affect the steps needed to find the difference?

iM KH

10.2: Try Clare's Algorithm

Clare used an algorithm to find the value of $538 - 156$.

Try using her algorithm to find the value of each difference.

$$\begin{array}{r} 4\ 13 \\ \cancel{5}\ \cancel{3}\ 8 \\ -\ 1\ 5\ 6 \\ \hline 3\ 8\ 2 \end{array}$$

1. $691 - 358$ = 333

2. $926 - 584$ = 342

3. $317 - 182$ = 135

4. $492 - 325$ = 167

Lesson 11: Analyze Subtraction Algorithms

- Let's think about subtraction algorithms in more detail.

Warm-up: Number Talk: Subtract within 1,000

Find the value of each expression mentally.

- 400 – 200 $= 200$

- 450 – 200 $= 250$

- 450 – 205 $= 245$

- 450 – 215 $= 235$

iM KH

11.1: Compare Two Subtraction Algorithms

1. The first steps of two algorithms are shown.

Algorithm A, step 1

$$
\begin{array}{r}
{\scriptstyle 4\ 10} \\
\cancel{5}\,\cancel{0}\,8 \\
-\ 1\ 5\ 6 \\
\hline
352
\end{array}
$$

Algorithm B, step 1

$$
\begin{array}{r}
5\ 0\ 8 \\
-\ 1\ 5\ 6 \\
\hline
35^2
\end{array}
$$

$500 + 00 + 8$
$100 + 50 + 6$

How are the steps different?

2. Use each algorithm to find the value of $824 - 541$.

$824 - 541 = 283$

$$
\begin{array}{r}
{\scriptstyle 7\ 12} \\
\cancel{8}\,\cancel{2}\,4 \\
-\ 5\ 4\ 1 \\
\hline
283
\end{array}
$$

$$
\begin{array}{r}
800 + 20 + 4 \\
-\ 500 + 40 + 1 \\
\hline
200 + 80 + 3
\end{array}
$$

11.2: Use an Algorithm?

Noah wanted to find the value of $301 - 167$ and wrote:

$$
\begin{array}{r}
3\ 0\ 1 \\
-\ 1\ 6\ 7 \\
\hline
\end{array}
$$

Elena said that we can't subtract this way because we would need more ones to subtract 7 ones, but there's a zero in the tens place of 301.

1. Do you agree with Elena's statement? Explain your reasoning.

_____

_____

2. Show how you would use an algorithm (either Noah's or another algorithm) to find the difference between 301 and 167.

Lesson 12: Subtract Strategically

- Let's consider when to use algorithms and when to use other strategies to subtract.

Warm-up: Number Talk: Threes

Find the value of each expression mentally.

- $2 \times 6 = 12$

- $3 \times 6 = 18$

- $2 \times 7 = 14$

- $3 \times 7 = 21$

$$\begin{array}{r} 400 \\ -\ 199 \\ \hline 301 \end{array}$$

$$\begin{array}{r} 602 \\ -\ 487 \\ \hline 115 \end{array}$$

12.1: How Would You Subtract?

Use a strategy or algorithm of your choice to find the value of each difference. Show your reasoning. Organize it so it can be followed by others.

1. $451 - 329 =$ 122

2. $382 - 190 =$ 192

3. $924 - 285 =$ 639

4. 600 – 478 = 122

5. 505 – 417

12.2: Greatest Difference, Smallest Difference

1. Decide with your partner whether you will try to make the greatest difference or smallest difference.

2. Take turns spinning and recording a digit in the hundreds, tens, or ones place. Continue until your numbers are complete.

3. Find the difference.

4. Compare your values.

5. Write a comparison using >, <, or =.

6. Play again.

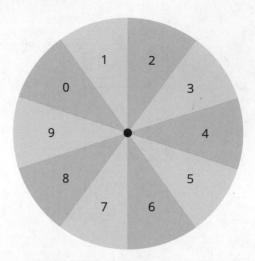

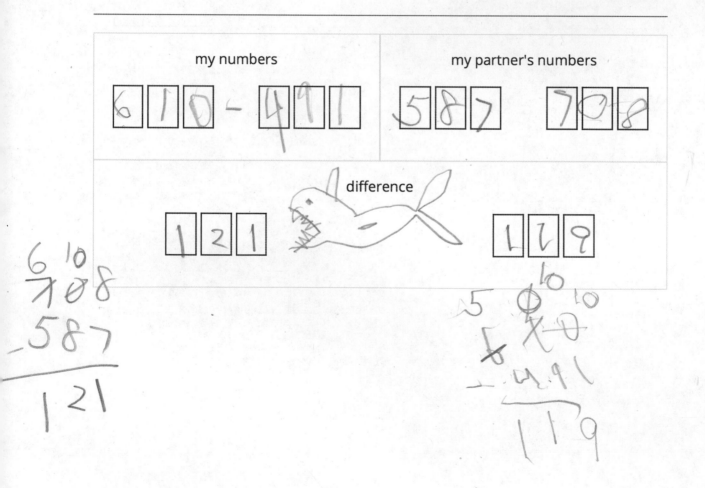

my numbers	my partner's numbers
610 − 491	587 708

difference

121   119

$\begin{array}{r} 6\,\overset{10}{\cancel{1}}\,\overset{}{8} \\ \cancel{7}\,\overset{}{0}\,8 \\ -5\,8\,7 \\ \hline 1\,2\,1 \end{array}$

$\begin{array}{r} \overset{}{5}\,\overset{10}{\cancel{0}}\,\overset{10}{\cancel{0}} \\ \cancel{7}\,\cancel{0}\,\cancel{0} \\ -\,4\,9\,1 \\ \hline 1\,1\,9 \end{array}$

iM KH

my numbers	my partner's numbers
☐☐☐ ☐☐☐	☐☐☐ ☐☐☐

difference

☐☐☐   ☐☐☐

---

my numbers	my partner's numbers
☐☐☐ ☐☐☐	☐☐☐ ☐☐☐

difference

☐☐☐   ☐☐☐

---

my numbers	my partner's numbers
☐☐☐ ☐☐☐	☐☐☐ ☐☐☐

difference

☐☐☐   ☐☐☐

Section B Summary

In this section, we learned algorithms to subtract numbers within 1,000. We also learned that we can choose whether to use an algorithm or another strategy for subtracting based on the numbers.

$$
\begin{array}{r}
\overset{400}{\cancel{500}} + \overset{130}{\cancel{30}} + 8 \\
-100 + 50 + 6 \\
\hline
300 + 80 + 2
\end{array}
$$

step 1

$$
\begin{array}{r}
5\ 3\ 8 \\
-\ 1\ 5\ 6 \\
\hline
2
\end{array}
$$

step 2

$$
\begin{array}{r}
{}^{4}{}^{13} \\
\cancel{5}\ \cancel{3}\ 8 \\
-\ 1\ 5\ 6 \\
\hline
2
\end{array}
$$

step 3

$$
\begin{array}{r}
{}^{4}{}^{13} \\
\cancel{5}\ \cancel{3}\ 8 \\
-\ 1\ 5\ 6 \\
\hline
8\ 2
\end{array}
$$

step 4

$$
\begin{array}{r}
{}^{4}{}^{13} \\
\cancel{5}\ \cancel{3}\ 8 \\
-\ 1\ 5\ 6 \\
\hline
3\ 8\ 2
\end{array}
$$

Section B Practice Problems

1. Find the value of $472 - 155$ in a way that makes sense to you.

(From Unit 3, Lesson 7.)

2. Here is a subtraction calculation.

$$
\begin{array}{c}
\ \ \overset{400}{\cancel{500}} + \overset{140}{\cancel{40}} + 5 \\
- 300 + 60 + 3 \\
\hline
\ \ 100 + 80 + 2
\end{array}
$$

a. Explain what the 400 above the 500 means.

_____

_____

b. Explain what the 140 above the 40 means.

_____

_____

c. Explain how the calculation works to find $545 - 363$.

_____

_____

(From Unit 3, Lesson 8.)

3. a. Write 518 and 346 in expanded form.

    b. Use the expanded form to find the difference of the two numbers.

    (From Unit 3, Lesson 9.)

4. a. Use an algorithm of your choice to find the value of $316 - 154$.

    b. Use an algorithm of your choice to find the value of $647 - 285$.

    (From Unit 3, Lesson 10.)

iM KH

5. Use an algorithm of your choice to find the value of each difference.

    a. $218 - 136$

    b. $473 - 258$

(From Unit 3, Lesson 11.)

6. Use a strategy or algorithm of your choice to find the value of each difference.

    a. $573 - 299$

    b. $653 - 341$

c. $371 - 158$

(From Unit 3, Lesson 12.)

7. **Exploration**

   Here is Noah's way to find the value of $523 - 371$.

   $$371 + 100 = 471$$
   $$471 + 30 = 501$$
   $$501 + 20 = 521$$
   $$521 + 2 = 523$$

   The answer is $100 + 30 + 20 + 2 = 152$.

   a. Explain why Noah's method works.

   _____

   _____

   b. Use Noah's method to calculate $618 - 266$.

iM KH

8. **Exploration**

a. Find the value of $600 - 253$. Explain or show your reasoning.

_____

_____

b. How is this problem different from other subtraction problems you have solved?

_____

_____

Section C: Round Within 1,000

Lesson 13: Multiples of 100

- Let's explore multiples of 100 and how other numbers relate to them.

Warm-up: Estimation Exploration: Marching Band

How many people are in the marching band?

Record an estimate that is:

too low	about right	too high

iM KH

13.1: About 100? Close to 100?

1. Here are the numbers of people in different parts of a school at noon during a school day.

   ○ playground: 94

   ○ cafeteria: 163

   ○ art room: 36

   ○ library: 13

   ○ classrooms: 216

   ○ gymnasium: 109

   ○ music room: 52

   Where in the school would you say that there are about 100 people?

   Record the numbers in the table. Be prepared to explain your reasoning.

about 100	not about 100

2. Now decide if the number of people in each part of the school is close to 0, close to 100, or close to 200.

   If you don't think a number belongs in any column, set it aside. Be prepared to explain your reasoning.

close to 0	close to 100	close to 200

13.2: Close to Multiples of 100

Your teacher will assign a set of numbers to you.

A	94	36	109	163	229
B	24	52	216	11	481
C	187	135	67	83	241
D	332	154	408	296	45
E	279	205	377	449	73

1. Work with your group to decide on which number line each number should go. Then, locate and label each number on the number line.

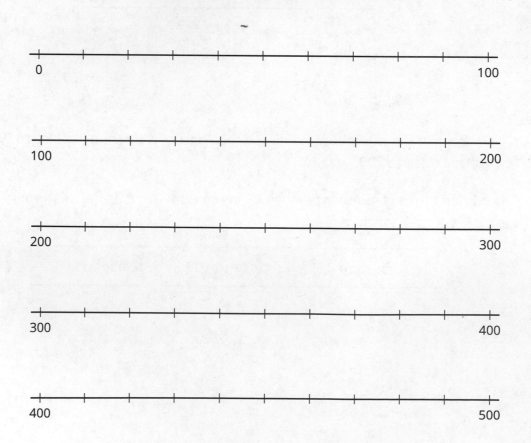

iM KH

2. Locate and label 364 on the correct number line.

    a. Name two multiples of 100 that are closest to 364.

    b. Of the two multiples of 100 you named, which one is 364 closer to?

3. Write the numbers assigned to you earlier. For each number, name the nearest multiple of 100.

number					
nearest multiple of 100					

Lesson 14: Nearest Multiples of 10 and 100

- For a given number, let's find the closest multiple of 100 and the closest multiple of 10.

Warm-up: Estimation Exploration: What Number Could this Be?

What number could the point on the number line represent?

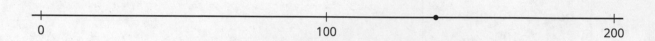

Record an estimate that is:

too low	about right	too high

iM KH

14.1: Close to Multiples of 10

1. a. Locate and label each number on a number line.

128   272   436   89   351

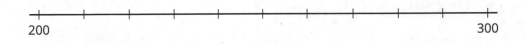

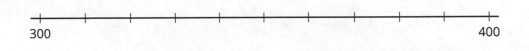

b. The same numbers are listed in the table. Name the multiple of 100 that is the nearest to each number. (Leave the last column blank for now.)

number	nearest multiple of 100	
128		
272		
436		
89		
351		

2. Look at the point for 128 on the number line.

    a. Name two multiples of 10 that are the closest to 128.

    b. Which of the two is the nearest multiple of 10?

3. Label the last column in the table "nearest multiple of 10." Then, name the nearest multiple of 10 for each number. Use the number lines if you find them helpful.

14.2: The Nearest Multiples

1. a. Is 349 closer to 300 or 400?

    b. Is 349 closer to 340 or 350?

2. a. Is 712 closer to 700 or 800?

    b. Is 712 closer to 710 or 720?

3. a. Is 568 closer to 500 or 600?

    b. Is 568 closer to 560 or 570?

4. Without locating a given number on a number line, how did you decide:

    a. the nearest multiple of 100?

    b. the nearest multiple of 10?

5. Name the nearest multiple of 100 and the nearest multiple of 10 for:

    a. 324

    b. 89

Lesson 15: Round to the Nearest Ten and Hundred

- Let's round to the nearest ten and hundred.

15.1: Can the Nearest Ten and Hundred be the Same?

1. Round each number to the nearest ten and the nearest hundred. Use number lines if you find them helpful.

number	nearest ten	nearest hundred
18	20	0
97	100	100
312	310	300
439	440	400
601	600	600

2. Kiran and Priya are rounding some numbers and are stuck when trying to round 415 and 750.

   ○ Kiran said, "415 doesn't have a nearest multiple of 10, so it can't be rounded to the nearest ten."

   ○ Priya said, "750 doesn't have a nearest multiple of 100, so it can't be rounded to the nearest hundred."

   Do you agree with Kiran and Priya? Explain your reasoning.

   _____

   _____

   _____

   _____

15.2: Round to Estimate

The table shows the numbers of people in different parts of a school at noon during a school day.

Andre and Lin are trying to estimate the number of people in the whole school. Andre plans to round the numbers to the nearest hundred. Lin plans to round them to the nearest ten.

1. Make a prediction: Whose estimate is going to be greater? Explain your reasoning.

   _____

   _____

2. Work with a partner to find Andre and Lin's estimates. Record them in the table. Then find the totals.

location	number	Andre's estimate (nearest hundred)	Lin's estimate (nearest ten)
playground	94		
cafeteria	163		
art room	36		
library	13		
classrooms	216		
gymnasium	109		
music room	52		
total			

3. Make two observations about the completed table. Was your prediction correct?

Lesson 16: Round and Round Again

Let's look for patterns in rounding.

Warm-up: Number Talk: More Groups, Fewer Groups

Find the value of each expression mentally.

- 5×7

- 4×7

- 6×7

- 4×8

16.1: All the Numbers

1. What are all the numbers that would round to 50 if you're rounding to the nearest ten? You can use this number line if it helps you.

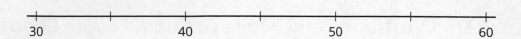

2. What are all the numbers that would round to 70 if you're rounding to the nearest ten?

3. What are all the numbers that would round to 600 if you're rounding to the nearest hundred?

If you finish early, find the numbers that would round to 100 and to 500 if you're rounding to the nearest hundred. Compare your lists with a partner's lists and discuss patterns you see.

iM KH

16.2: What's My Mystery Number?

Write down a number between 100 and 1,000 on your index card. This is your mystery number.

Fold your index card in half so that no one can see your mystery number.

Write down 3 clues about your mystery number by finishing these sentences:

1. My mystery number is (odd or even) _____.

2. My mystery number rounds to _____.

3. My mystery number is between _____ and _____.

Play What's My Number?

1. Read the clues for your mystery number.

2. Starting with the person on your right, have every member in your team try to guess your mystery number and explain their reasoning.

3. If they haven't guessed the mystery number by the time the last person shares, reveal the mystery number.

4. Repeat steps 1 through 3 with the next person in the group reading the clues for their mystery number.

Section C Summary

In this section, we learned that rounding is a formal way to decide what number a given number is closest to. We rounded numbers to the nearest ten and the nearest hundred. We saw that a number line can help us see the closest multiple of 10 or 100.

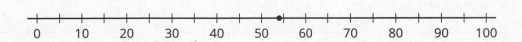

Section C Practice Problems

1. a. Locate and label 539 on one of the number lines.

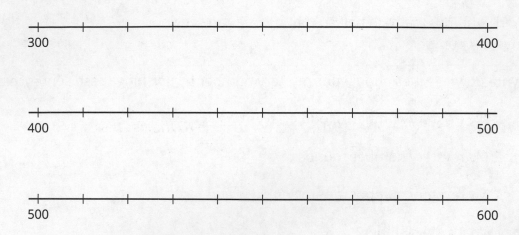

   b. What is the closest multiple of 100 to 539?

   (From Unit 3, Lesson 13.)

2. Find the nearest multiple of 10 and the nearest multiple of 100 for:

   a. 537

   b. 661

   (From Unit 3, Lesson 14.)

3. a. What are all the numbers that round to 350 when rounded to the nearest 10?

   b. Which numbers round to 350 when rounded to the nearest ten and round to 400 when rounded to the nearest hundred?

   (From Unit 3, Lesson 16.)

iM KH

4. a. What is 346 rounded to the nearest ten? Explain or show your reasoning.

    b. What is 346 rounded to the nearest hundred? Explain or show your reasoning.

(From Unit 3, Lesson 15.)

5. Round each number to the nearest ten and to the nearest hundred. Explain or show your reasoning.

    a. 254

    b. 145

(From Unit 3, Lesson 15.)

6. Jada rounds 145 to the nearest ten and gets 150. Then she rounds 150 to the nearest hundred and gets 200. Jada says 145 rounded to the nearest hundred is 200. Do you agree with Jada? Explain or show your reasoning.

7. **Exploration**

    It is 234 miles from New York City to Boston. Tyler says, "That's about 200 miles, so it's about 400 miles to travel back and forth between New York City and Boston." Do you agree with Tyler? Explain or show your reasoning.

Section D: Solve Two-Step Problems

Lesson 17: Does It Make Sense?

- Let's decide if our answers make sense.

Warm-up: True or False: Is it Greater?

Decide if each statement is true or false. Be prepared to explain your reasoning.

$132 + 115 > 200$

$228 + 195 > 400$

$217 + 151 > 400$

iM KH

17.1: Quick Estimates

1. There are 212 beads in a plastic bag. Then, 98 of the beads are used to make a necklace. Finally, 308 beads are placed in the bag.

   Priya makes an estimate that there are about 400 beads in the bag now. Does Priya's estimate make sense? Explain your reasoning.

   $212 - 98 = 114$ $114 + 308$

   $= 422$ It is not 422

   but it is not exzacky 400

2. Estimate the answer for each of these problems.

   a. Clare has 252 beads. She used 92 beads to make some bracelets. Then, a friend gave her 203 beads. How many beads does Clare have now?

   363   $252 - 92 = 160$

   $160 + 203 = 363$

   b. Han had 558 beads. His sister had 302 beads. They combined their beads for an art project that used 250 beads. How many beads do they have left?

   610

   $558 + 302 = 860$

   $860 - 250 = 610$

17.2: Solve and Reason

1. Solve one of the problems. Explain or show your reasoning.

   a. Jada has 326 beads. She gives her friend 32 beads. Then, Jada uses 84 beads to make a bracelet for her cousin. How many beads does Jada have now?

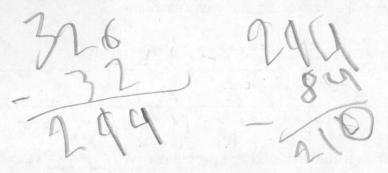

$$
\begin{array}{r}
326 \\
-\ 32 \\
\hline
294
\end{array}
$$

$$
\begin{array}{r}
294 \\
84 \\
\hline
-\ 210
\end{array}
$$

   b. Noah starts an art project on Monday and uses 624 beads. On Tuesday he uses 132 more beads. Finally, on Wednesday he finishes the project by using 48 more beads. How many beads did Noah use on his art project?

2. Trade work with a partner. Decide whether your partner's answer for their problem makes sense. On their paper, explain your reasoning.

_____

_____

_____

_____

iM KH

Lesson 18: Diagrams and Equations for Word Problems

- Let's connect diagrams and equations to situations.

Warm-up: Notice and Wonder: Diagrams

What do you notice? What do you wonder?

40 + 20 = 60

142	20

162?

| 5 | 5 | 5 | 5 |

20?

5 × 4 = 20

142	5	5	5	5

162?

5 × 4 + 142 = 162

18.1: Card Sort: Situations, Equations, and Diagrams

Your teacher will give you a set of cards showing situations, equations, and diagrams.

Sort the cards into groups so that the cards in each group represent the same situation. Be ready to explain your reasoning.

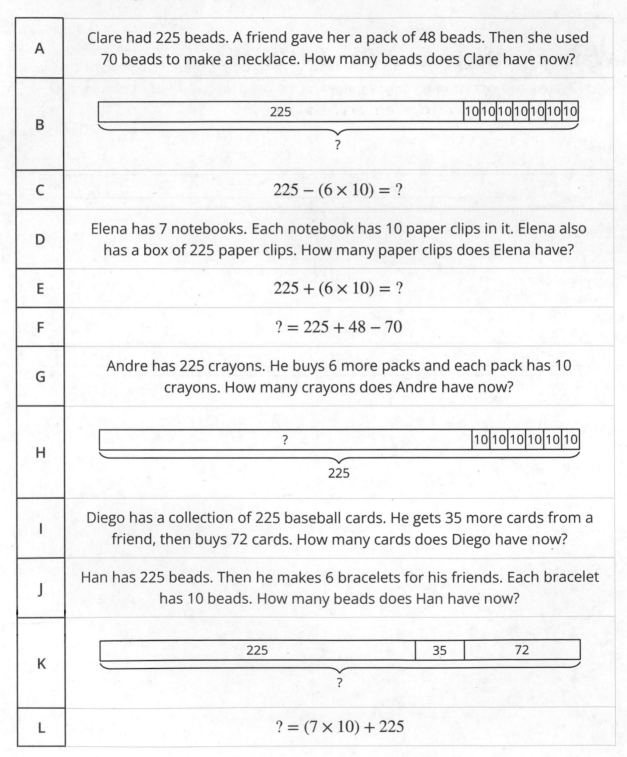

A	Clare had 225 beads. A friend gave her a pack of 48 beads. Then she used 70 beads to make a necklace. How many beads does Clare have now?
B	225 ... 10 10 10 10 10 10 10 ?
C	$225 - (6 \times 10) = ?$
D	Elena has 7 notebooks. Each notebook has 10 paper clips in it. Elena also has a box of 225 paper clips. How many paper clips does Elena have?
E	$225 + (6 \times 10) = ?$
F	$? = 225 + 48 - 70$
G	Andre has 225 crayons. He buys 6 more packs and each pack has 10 crayons. How many crayons does Andre have now?
H	? ... 10 10 10 10 10 10 ... 225
I	Diego has a collection of 225 baseball cards. He gets 35 more cards from a friend, then buys 72 cards. How many cards does Diego have now?
J	Han has 225 beads. Then he makes 6 bracelets for his friends. Each bracelet has 10 beads. How many beads does Han have now?
K	225 35 72 ?
L	$? = (7 \times 10) + 225$

iM KH

18.2: Makes Sense to Me: A Gallery Walk

1. Your teacher will assign a problem to your group. Work together to solve your assigned problem.

2. Create a poster of your group's solution. Organize your work so that it can be followed by others.

3. As you visit other groups' posters, consider how each answer makes sense.

   Choose one poster and make a comment on the solution. Write on your sticky note how you know the answer makes sense.

Lesson 19: Situations and Equations

- Let's represent and solve problems.

Warm-up: Notice and Wonder: The Unknown

What do you notice? What do you wonder?

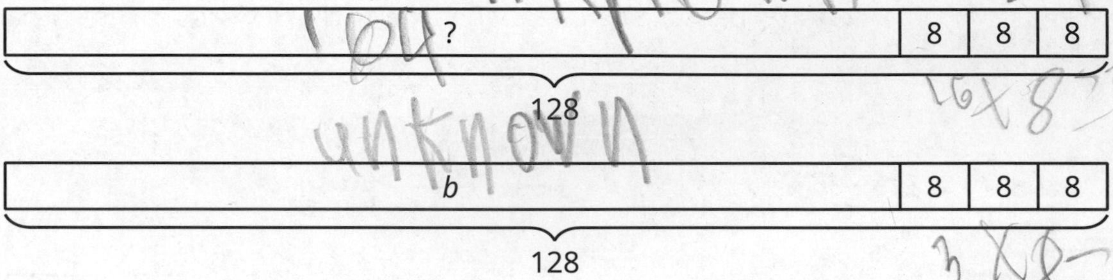

[Handwritten annotations: "unknown 24", "8+8=24", "unknown", "24", "3x8=24", "both have a total of 128"]

	?		8	8	8

128

	b		8	8	8

128

19.1: Mai's Beads

Part 1

Match each diagram with a situation. Be ready to explain your reasoning.

- Situation 1: Mai had 104 beads. She bought two packs of beads and now she has 124 beads. How many beads were in each pack?

- Situation 2: Mai had some beads. She bought 2 more packs of beads and each pack has 10 beads in it. Now she has 124 beads. How many beads did Mai have before?

- Situation 3: Mai had 104 beads. She bought 2 more packs of beads and each pack has 10 beads in it. How many beads does she have now?

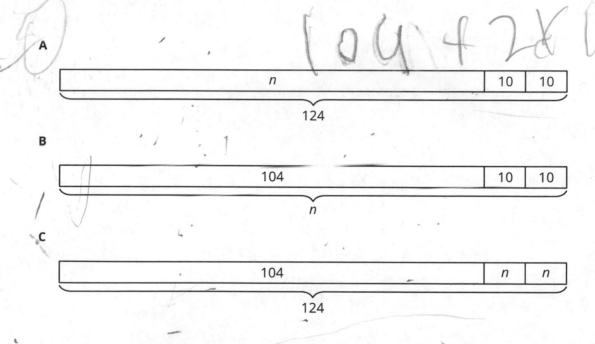

Part 2

Match each equation with a letter for the unknown quantity to a situation in Part 1.

1. $104 + 2 \times 10 = n$

2. $104 + (2 \times n) = 124$

3. $n + 10 + 10 = 124$

19.2: Represent, Solve, Explain

Kiran is setting up a game of mancala. He has a jar of 104 stones.

From the jar, he takes 3 stones for each of the 6 pits on his side of the board.

How many stones are in the jar now?

1. Write an equation to represent the situation. Use a letter for the unknown quantity.

2. Solve the problem. Explain or show your reasoning.

3. Explain how you know your answer makes sense.

_____

_____

Lesson 20: More Practice to Represent and Solve

- Let's represent and solve more problems.

Warm-up: Number Talk: Two Steps

Find the value of each expression mentally.

- $20 + (2 \times 3)$

- $30 + (4 \times 3)$

- $50 + (8 \times 3)$

- $99 + (8 \times 3)$

20.1: Info Gap: Introduction

Problem Card

A room has some chairs set up in rows and some chairs stacked up in a corner.

How many chairs are in the room?

20.2: Info Gap: Bake Sale

Your teacher will give you either a problem card or a data card. Do not show or read your card to your partner.

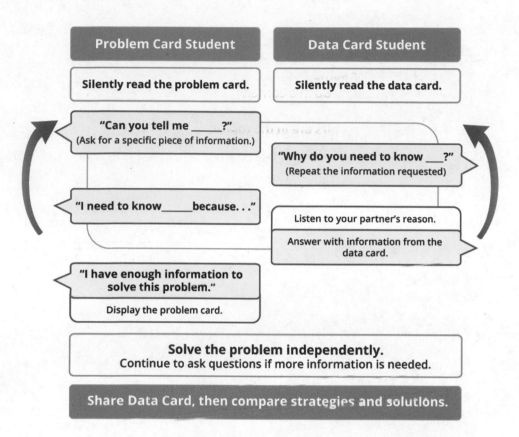

Pause here so your teacher can review your work.

Ask your teacher for a new set of cards and repeat the activity, trading roles with your partner.

Section D Summary

In this section, we used rounding to estimate answers to problems. This helped us decide if our answers to problems made sense based on the situation and the numbers in the situation.

We also wrote equations with an unknown and used diagrams to solve for the exact answer in problems.

Situation:

Mai had 104 beads. She bought 2 more packs of beads and each pack has 10 beads in it. How many beads does she have now?

Diagram:

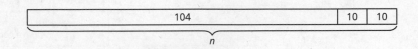

Equation with an unknown:

$$104 + (2 \times 10) = n$$

Lesson 21: Classroom Supplies

- Let's make a wish list for class supplies.

Warm-up: Notice and Wonder: School Supplies List

What do you notice? What do you wonder?

work supplies	cost
box of 25 markers	$5
box of 100 crayons	$8

class library	cost
set of 20 books about history	$250
story book (80 to choose from)	$8

special items	cost
carpet for the reading corner	$65
a class aquarium, with fish	$159

entertainment	cost
board games (40 to choose from)	$15
interactive computer games (math and reading)	$75

21.1: Make a Wish List

Imagine our class received $1,000 to spend on school supplies from the given list. How would you spend the money to benefit our classroom the most?

work supplies	cost
box of 25 markers	$5
box of 100 crayons	$8
box of 60 pencils	$5
box of 5,000 pages of printer paper	$40
package of 10 pads of lined paper	$15
box of 50 pieces of construction paper	$32

class library	cost
set of 20 books about history	$250
set of books about nature	$400
story book (80 choices)	$8
maps (5 choices: world, continent, North America, U.S. state, U.S. city)	$45

special items	cost
carpet for the reading corner	$65
a class aquarium, with fish	$150
fish food for one month	$15
field trip to the zoo	$350

entertainment	cost
puzzles (30 choices)	$12
board games (40 choices)	$15
interactive computer games (math and reading)	$75

iM KH

1. Make a plan on how to spend the money. You may purchase more than one of the same item. Use estimation or rounding to keep track of the total as you make your selections.

2. On your wish list, what is the total cost of the items in each category?

   ○ Supplies   ○ Puzzles and games

   ○ Books and maps   ○ Special items

3. What was the total cost of all your choices?

   a. Would you have any money left over? If so, how much?

   b. Did you spend too much money? If so, how much?

21.2: What's on Your List?

1. Share your wish list with another group. Take turns to explain how you made your choices and listen to the choices of the other group.

2. Compare your spending:

   ◦ How much more or less did you choose to spend on each category than the other group?

   ◦ How much more or less did you spend in total compared to your partner group?

Section D Practice Problems

1. There are 708 students at the school. Three hundred ninety-four students are in the cafeteria and the rest are in class. Han estimates that 400 students are in class. Do you agree with Han's estimate? Explain or show your reasoning.

(From Unit 3, Lesson 17.)

2. Select **all** equations that match the tape diagram.

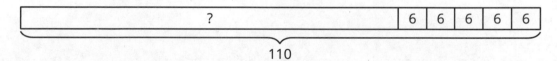

   A. $110 + 5 \times 6 = ?$

   B. $? + 5 \times 6 = 110$

   C. $110 - ? = 5 \times 6$

   D. $110 + ? = 5 \times 6$

   E. $110 - 30 = ?$

(From Unit 3, Lesson 18.)

3. There are 240 connecting cubes in the box. Five students each take 9 connecting cubes from the box. How many connecting cubes are left in the box?

   a. Write an equation to represent the situation. Use a letter for the unknown quantity.

   b. Solve the problem. Explain or show your reasoning.

(From Unit 3, Lesson 19.)

4. Andre has 245 cards. He bought 7 more packages of cards. How many cards does he have now?

   a. What information do you need to know to answer the question?

   b. Write an expression to represent the situation. Use a letter for the unknown quantity.

(From Unit 3, Lesson 20.)

5. **Exploration**

   For each equation, draw a diagram and write a situation with a question.

   a. $3 \times n + 163 = 187$

b. $b - (4 \times 10) = 89$

6. **Exploration**

   a. A question in a subtraction situation can be answered with an estimate of "about 200." What could the subtraction situation be?

   b. A question in a situation that uses addition and multiplication could be answered with an estimate of "about 300." What could the situation be?

iM KH

GRADE 3
Unit

4

Student Edition Units 3-4

Certified by Illustrative Mathematics®

Section A: What is Division?

Lesson 1: How Many Groups?

- Let's represent and solve problems.

Warm-up: How Many Do You See: Apples

How many do you see? How do you see them?

4 × 4 = 16

1.1: How Many Apples?

Solve each problem. Show your thinking using objects, a drawing, or a diagram.

1. If 24 apples are put into boxes with 8 apples in each box, how many boxes are there?

2. If 42 apples are put into boxes with 6 apples in each box, how many boxes are there?

3. If 32 apples are put into boxes with 4 apples in each box, how many boxes are there?

1.2: Gallery Walk: Apples in Boxes

1. Visit the posters around the room with your partner. Discuss what is the same and what is different about the thinking shown on each poster.

2. Reflect on what you saw. Write down one thing that was the same and one thing that was different about the thinking shown on each poster.

_____

_____

_____

_____

_____

_____

_____

Lesson 2: How Many in Each Group?

- Let's represent and solve more problems.

Warm-up: Notice and Wonder: More Apples

What do you notice? What do you wonder?

iM KH

2.1: How Many Apples?

Solve each problem. Show your thinking using objects, a drawing, or a diagram.

1. If 20 apples are packed into 4 boxes with each box having the same number of apples, how many apples are in each box?

$5 \times 4 = 20$ $20 \div 4 = 5$

2. If 36 apples are packed into 6 boxes with each box having the same number of apples, how many apples are in each box?

$36 \div 6 = 6$

3. If 45 apples are packed into 9 boxes with each box having the same number of apples, how many apples are in each box?

$9 \times 5 = 45$ $45 \div 9 = 5$

2.2: Gallery Walk

Visit the posters around the room with your partner. Discuss what is the same and what is different about the thinking shown on each poster.

2.3: All the Apples

If 24 apples are put into boxes with 8 apples in each box, how many boxes are there?

If 20 apples are packed into 4 boxes with each box having the same number of apples, how many apples are in each box?

Discuss with your partner:

- How are these problems alike?

- How are they different?

- What is alike and what is different about how these problems are represented and solved?

Lesson 3: Division Situation Drawings

- Let's represent division situations with drawings.

Warm-up: Number Talk: The More Things Change...

Find the value of each expression mentally.

- 120 + 120
- 121 + 119
- 125 + 115
- 129 + 111

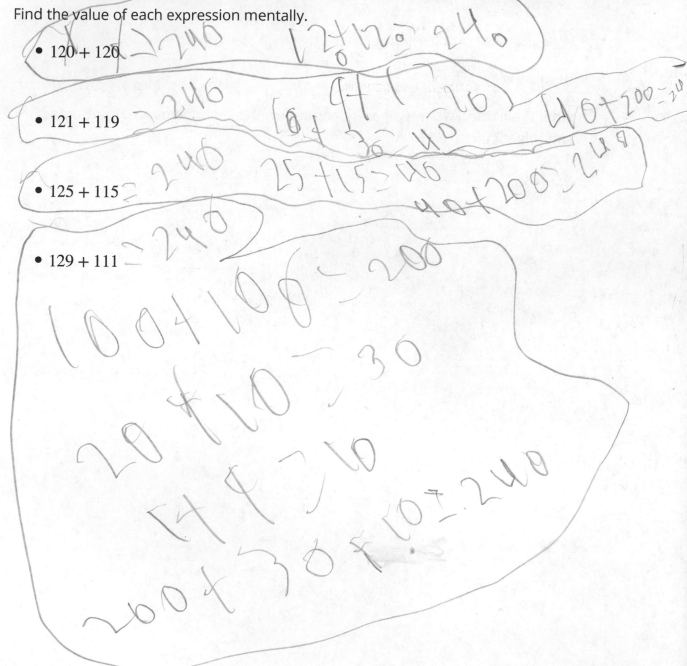

3.1: Groups of Students

1. What did you notice about how the students put themselves into groups of 2?

2. What did you notice about how the students put themselves into 2 groups?

3.2: Elena's Colored Pencils

Elena has 12 colored pencils. She has 2 boxes and wants to put the same number of colored pencils in each box. How many colored pencils will go in each box?

Which drawing matches the situation? Explain your reasoning.

A

B

The second that's not two boxs. I has 12 pens and two boxs.

3.3: Which Drawing Matches?

Match each situation to a drawing. Be prepared to explain your reasoning.

1. Mai has 8 markers. She puts 4 markers in each box. How many boxes of markers are there?

A

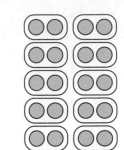

2. Kiran has 20 pens. He puts 2 pens at each table. How many tables can he put pens on?

B

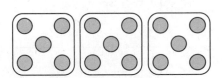

3. Lin has 8 colored pencils. She puts them into 2 bags. Each bag has the same number of colored pencils. How many colored pencils will be in each bag?

C

4. Priya has 15 crayons. She puts 5 crayons on each desk. How many desks will have crayons?

5. Noah has 20 pencils. He puts the same number of pencils into 10 boxes. How many pencils will be in each box?

6. Jada has 15 markers. She puts the same number of markers on 3 tables. How many markers will be on each table?

Lesson 4: Interpret Division Expressions

- Let's make sense of division expressions.

Warm-up: Number Talk: More or Less?

Find the value of each expression mentally.

- 500 − 475 $= 25$

- 504 − 475 $= 29$

- 512 − 475 $= 37$

- 512 − 449 $= 63$

$$\begin{array}{r} 500 \\ -475 \\ \hline 255 \end{array} \qquad \begin{array}{r} 509 \\ -975 \\ \hline 29 \end{array} \qquad \begin{array}{r} 512 \\ -425 \\ \hline 37 \end{array}$$

$$\begin{array}{r} 512 \\ -449 \\ \hline 63 \end{array}$$

iM KH

4.1: Spinning Tops

Spinning tops are popular around the world. Here are spinning tops from a few different cultures.

Match each situation about spinning tops with an expression that can represent it.

1. Clare has a collection of 24 spinning tops in four colors. She has the same number of tops in black, white, red, and green. How many tops of each color does she have?

24 X 6 = 24

A. 24 ÷ 2 = 12

2. Priya and her friend are decorating 24 wooden tops with paint. If each person is painting the same number of tops, how many tops is each person painting?

2 X 12 = 24

B. 12 ÷ 2 = 6

3. A store has 24 tops from around the world displayed in 6 boxes. Each box contains the same number of tops. How many tops are in each box?

6 X 4 = 24

C. 24 ÷ 4 = 6

4. Diego has 12 trompos that he wants to give as gifts. If he gives each friend 2 trompos, how many friends can get them as gifts?

2 X 6 = 12

D. 12 ÷ 6 = 2

5. Six friends are playing with 12 dreidels. If everyone is playing with the same number of dreidels, how many dreidels does each person have?

6 X 2 = 12

E. 24 ÷ 6 = 4

4.2: Cars in Boxes

Consider these two situations.

A. Han has 21 toy cars. He puts the same number of cars in each of 3 boxes. How many cars will be in each box?

B. Han has 21 toy cars. He wants to put 3 cars in each box. How many boxes will he need?

Which situation does the expression 21 ÷ 3 represent? Explain your reasoning.

_____

_____

_____

_____

iM KH

4.3: Stacks of Blocks

Match each situation to a drawing and an expression that represent the situation. Be prepared to explain your reasoning.

1. Kiran uses 6 blocks to make stacks. Each stack has 2 blocks. How many stacks are there?

2. Han uses 6 blocks to make two equal stacks. How many blocks are in each stack?

3. Jada uses 6 blocks to build stacks with 3 blocks each. How many stacks are there?

4. Mai uses 6 blocks to make 3 equal stacks. How many blocks are in each stack?

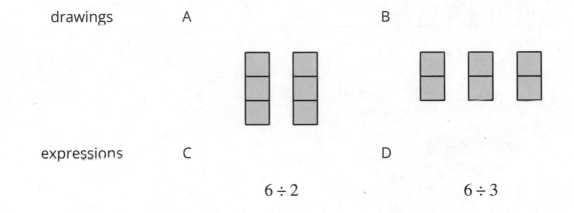

drawings   A   B

expressions   C   D

$$6 \div 2 \qquad\qquad 6 \div 3$$

Lesson 5: Write Division Expressions

- Let's write division expressions and solve "how many groups?" and "how many in each group?" problems.

Warm-up: Number Talk: What's the Same?

Find the value of each expression mentally.

- 225 – 100

- 227 – 102

- 230 – 105

- 220 – 95

iM KH

5.1: Card Sort: All about Bugs

1. Your teacher will give you a set of cards that show situations. Sort the cards into 2 categories of your choosing. Be prepared to explain the meaning of your categories.

A. Mole crickets have special legs for digging. Ten special legs belong to 5 mole crickets. How many special legs does each mole cricket have?

B. A beetle has a pair of antennae for sensing heat, touch, smell, and more. If there are 8 antennae, how many beetles are there?

C. Fourteen antennae belong to a group of bees. If each bee has 2 antennae, how many bees are there?

D. There are 12 wings. If each dragonfly has 4 wings, how many dragonflies are there?

E. Thirty legs belong to 5 ants. If all the ants have the same number of legs, how many legs does each ant have?

F. There are 50 spots on 5 butterflies. If each butterfly has the same number of spots, how many spots does each butterfly have?

2. Write a division expression to represent each situation. Be ready to explain your reasoning.

5.2: Solve a Buggy Problem

Your teacher will assign a problem to your group.

Create a visual display that shows your thinking and your solution to the problem.

Section A Summary

In this section, we learned that division is finding the number of groups or finding the size of each group when we put objects into groups of equal size. We represented division situations with drawings and expressions, and solved division problems.

"How many groups?"   "How many in each group?"

Han has 12 colored pencils. He wants to put 2 colored pencils in each box until he's out of colored pencils. How many boxes does Han need?

Elena has 12 colored pencils. She has 2 boxes and wants to put the same number of colored pencils in each box. How many pencils will be in each box?

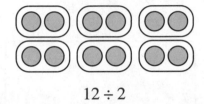

$12 \div 2$

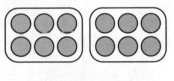

$12 \div 2$

Section A Practice Problems

1. Pre-unit

a. Write a multiplication expression that represents the array.

b. Write a multiplication equation that represents the array.

4×5=20 *0*

2. Pre-unit

Find the area of each rectangle.

A

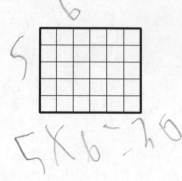

5 *6* *5×6=30*

B

10 cm

4 cm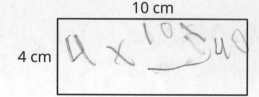

4 × 10 = 40

3. Pre-unit

The area of the rectangle is 40 square centimeters.

Find the missing side length of the rectangle. Explain your reasoning.

5 cm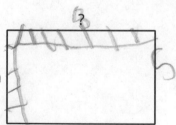

5 × 8 = 40   50 − 10 8 40

5×8 = 10

124

4. **Pre-unit**

Find the number that makes each equation true.

a. $8 \times 5 =$ __40__

b. $5 \times$ __7__ $= 35$

c. __9__ $\times 2 = 18$

5. **Pre-unit**

There are 6 volleyball teams in the gym. Each team has 10 players. How many volleyball players are there altogether?

a. Make a drawing of the situation.

b. Write an equation with a "?" for the unknown that represents the situation.

c. Solve the problem.

6. For each problem, show your thinking using a drawing or a diagram.

a. There are 40 apples packed into boxes. If there are 8 apples in each box, how many boxes are there?

b. There are 40 apples packed into boxes. If there are 10 apples in each box, how many boxes are there?

(From Unit 4, Lesson 1.)

7. For each problem, show your thinking using a drawing or a diagram.

    a. There are 30 oranges. If they are packed into 5 bags with the same amount of oranges in each bag, how many oranges are in each bag?

    b. There are 30 oranges. If they are packed into 3 bags with the same amount of oranges in each bag, how many oranges are in each bag?

(From Unit 4, Lesson 2.)

8. a. 10 people go to the movies in cars. Two people go in each car. How many cars are there? Show your thinking using a drawing or a diagram.

    b. 10 other people go to the movies in cars. They ride in 2 cars with the same number in each car. How many people are in each car? Show your thinking using a drawing or diagram.

    c. How are the two situations the same? How are they different? How are the diagrams the same? How are they different?

(From Unit 4, Lesson 3.)

9. There are 20 desks in the class. They are divided equally into 5 groups. How many desks are in each group?

    a. Which expression represents this situation: $20 \div 4$ or $20 \div 5$? Explain your reasoning.

    _____

    _____

b. Choose the diagram that represents this situation. Explain your reasoning.

A

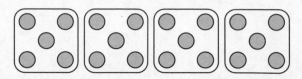

B

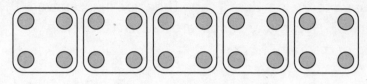

_____

_____

(From Unit 4, Lesson 4.)

10. Mai's family picked 40 pounds of peaches. They put 5 pounds in each bag.

    a. Write a division expression that represents the situation.

    b. How many bags of peaches did Mai's family pick? Explain or show your reasoning.

(From Unit 4, Lesson 5.)

11. Complete each story by putting a number in the blank that makes sense. Then, answer the questions. Draw a diagram to solve each problem.

    a. Mai has _____ stickers. She is going to put the same number of stickers on each of her 5 notebooks. How many stickers will be on each notebook?

iM KH

b. Andre has _____ cards. He is going to arrange them in rows of _____ cards. How many rows will Andre's cards make?

12. **Exploration**

   Write a division situation to match each diagram.

   A

   B

   C

Section B: Relate Multiplication and Division

Lesson 6: Division as an Unknown Factor

- Let's connect division equations to multiplication equations.

Warm-up: Notice and Wonder: Missing Numbers

What do you notice? What do you wonder?

$$3 \times \text{?} = 12 \qquad\qquad 12 \div 3 = \text{?}$$

iM KH

6.1: Equations about Onions

A farmer puts 14 onions into 2 bags, with the same number of onions in each bag.

Lin says the situation should be represented by the equation:

$$2 \times \boxed{} = 14$$

Mai says the situation should be represented by the equation:

$$14 \div 2 = \boxed{}$$

Whose equation do you agree with? Be ready to explain your reasoning.

6.2: At the Farmers' Market

Complete each row. Be prepared to explain your reasoning.

situation	drawing or diagram	multiplication equation	division equation
Elena's family buys 18 avocados at the farmers market. The avocados are in bags of 3 each.			$18 \div 3 = \underline{\quad}$
Andre sees 25 tomatoes. They are in 5 bunches. Each bunch has the same number of tomatoes.		$5 \times ? = 25$	$25 \div 5 = ?$
Lin orders 6 banana fritters. The fritters are served on 2 plates and each plate has the same number of fritters.		$2 \times ? = 6$	
		$\underline{\quad} \times 10 = 30$	$30 \div 10 = \underline{\quad}$

132

iM KH

Lesson 7: Relate Multiplication and Division

• Let's make more connections between multiplication and division.

Warm-up: How Many Do You See: Tens

How many do you see? How do you see them?

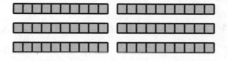

7.1: Division Round Table

Your teacher will give you a sheet of paper with 4 boxes on it and instruct you to draw or write something in each box.

After working on each box, pause and wait for your teacher's instructions for the next box.

1. Draw equal groups in Box 1 on your recording sheet.

2. In Box 2, write a description of a division situation that matches the drawing you just received.

3. In Box 3, write a multiplication equation that matches the drawing and division situation you just received. Use a symbol for the unknown quantity.

4. In Box 4, write a division equation that matches the drawing, division situation, and multiplication equation you just received. Use a symbol for the unknown quantity.

iM KH

7.2: Sets of School Supplies

For each situation:

a. Write an equation with a symbol for the unknown quantity to represent the situation.

b. Solve the problem and find the unknown number in the equation. Be prepared to explain your reasoning.

1. Kiran had 32 paper clips. He gave each student 4 paper clips. How many students received paper clips?

    a. Equation: _____

    b.

2. There are 28 books in 4 stacks. If each stack has the same amount of books, how many books are in each stack?

    a. Equation: _____

    b.

3. There are 6 boxes. Each box has 8 erasers. How many erasers are there?

    a. Equation: _____

    b.

4. Lin had 36 sticky notes. She placed 6 sticky notes on each notebook. How many notebooks received sticky notes?

    a. Equation: _____

    b.

Lesson 8: Relate Quotients to Familiar Products

- Let's consider the products and quotients we know right away or can find quickly.

Warm-up: Number Talk: Multiplication and Division

Find the value of each expression mentally.

- 4×10

- $40 \div 4$

- $40 \div 10$

- $60 \div 6$

iM KH

8.1: Card Sort: Multiplication

Quiz your partner on their multiplication facts. Sort your partner's facts into one of these columns:

1. know it right away

2. can find it quickly

3. don't know it yet

Multiplication expressions I'm going to practice:

1.

2.

3.

4.

5.

8.2: If I Know, Then I Know

If I know $4 \times 5 = 20$, then I know _____.

1. Set the multiplication fact cards in a stack face down.

2. Take turns drawing a multiplication fact card.

3. Use the multiplication fact on the card to record a multiplication equation in the "If I know . . ." column.

4. Then, record related division equations in the "Then I know . . ." column.

If I know . . . ,	then I know . . .

iM KH

Lesson 9: Patterns in the Multiplication Table

- Let's find patterns in the multiplication table and use them to multiply.

Warm-up: Notice and Wonder: Multiplication Table

What do you notice? What do you wonder?

×	1	2	3	4	5
1	1	2	3	4	5
2	2	4	6	8	10
3	3	6	9	12	15
4	4	8	12	16	20
5	5	10	15	20	25

9.1: Products in the Table

Here is a partially completed multiplication table.

×	1	2	3	4	5	6	7	8	9	10
1	1	2	3	4	5					
2	2	4	6	8	10		A			
3	3	6	9	12	15				B	
4	4	8	12	16	20	C				
5	5	10	15	20	25			D		
6	6	12	18	24	30					E
7	7	14	21	28	35		F			
8	8	16	24	32	40	48			G	
9	9	18	27	36	45	54	63			
10	10	20	30	40	50	60	70	80		

1. Use the products in the table to help you find the numbers that should replace letters A–G. Be prepared to explain your reasoning.

2. Find the number that should go in three other empty cells in the table. Use:

   a. 7 as a factor

   b. 9 as a factor

   c. 10 as a factor

   Be prepared to explain your reasoning.

iM KH

9.2: If I Know, Then I Know: Multiplication

1. In each row, write down at least two multiplication facts you can figure out because you know the given multiplication fact in the left column. Be prepared to share your reasoning.

If I know . . . ,	then I also know . . .
2×4	$4 \times 2, 4 \times 4, 2 \times 8$
3×5	
4×10	
7×2	
5×8	

2. If time permits, complete the rest of the multiplication table. Use the multiplication facts you know to find those you don't know.

Lesson 10: Explore Multiplication Strategies with Rectangles

- Let's use rectangles to explore multiplication strategies.

Warm-up: How Many Do You See: Squares

How many do you see? How do you see them?

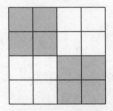

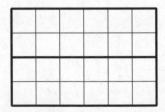

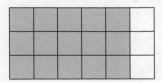

iM KH

10.1: From Diagrams to Expressions

Andre and Elena are finding the area of this rectangle.

Andre writes 6×3.　　He marks the rectangle like this:　　He then writes:

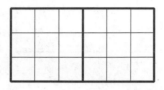

$2 \times (3 \times 3)$
$2 \times 9 = 18$

Elena writes 3×6.　　She marks the rectangle like this:　　She then writes:

$3 \times (5 + 1)$
$(3 \times 5) + (3 \times 1)$
$15 + 3$
18

1. Discuss with a partner:

   a. How are Andre and Elena's strategies alike? How are they different?

   b. How are the numbers in Andre's expressions related to his diagram?

   c. How are the numbers in Elena's expressions related to her diagram?

2. Here is another rectangle.

   Its area can be found by finding 4×9.

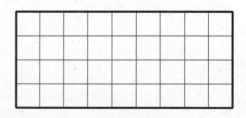

   a. Mark or shade the rectangle in a way that would help you find its area.

   b. Write one or more expressions that can represent your work on the diagram and show how you find the area.

10.2: From Expressions to Diagrams

Here are some rectangles and expressions that show how three students saw the area of the rectangles.

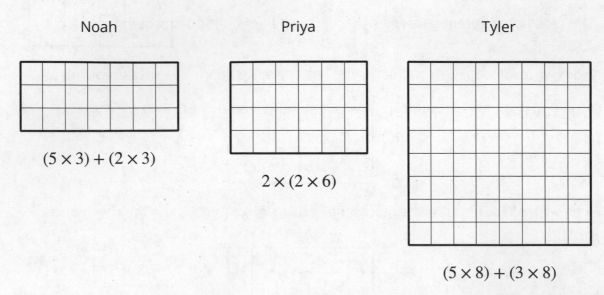

Noah

$(5 \times 3) + (2 \times 3)$

Priya

$2 \times (2 \times 6)$

Tyler

$(5 \times 8) + (3 \times 8)$

For each rectangle:

1. Name the two factors that can be multiplied to find its area.

2. Mark or shade each rectangle to show how each student saw the area. Be prepared to explain your reasoning.

iM KH

Lesson 11: Multiplication Strategies on Ungridded Rectangles

- Let's use different strategies to find the area of ungridded rectangles.

Warm-up: Which One Doesn't Belong: Multiplication in Many Forms

Which one doesn't belong?

A

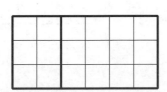

B

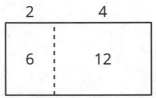

C

$(3 \times 2) + (3 \times 4)$

D

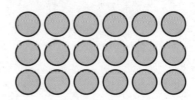

11.1: Mark, then Express

For each rectangle:

- Mark or shade each rectangle to show a strategy for finding its area.

- Write one or more expressions that can represent how you find the area.

A

9
5

B

6
6

C

8
7

iM KH

11.2: Card Sort: Different Expressions, Same Rectangle

Your teacher will give you a set of cards with expressions that represent areas of rectangles.

Sort the expressions into groups so that the expressions in each group can represent the area of the same rectangle. Be prepared to explain your reasoning.

You can draw rectangles if you find them helpful.

A $(7 \times 2) \times 2$	B 6×7	C 7×4	D 8×3
E $3 \times 6 + 5 \times 6$	F $(4 \times 3) \times 2$	G $4 \times (2 \times 3)$	H 4×9
I $(5 \times 6) + (2 \times 6)$	J $2 \times (2 \times 9)$	K 8×6	L $(5 \times 4) + (2 \times 4)$

Section B Summary

In this section, we learned how multiplication and division are related.

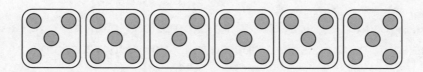

$$6 \times 5 = ? \qquad 30 \div 5 = ? \qquad 30 \div 6 = ?$$

We used strategies to multiply and divide and worked towards fluent multiplication and division within 100.

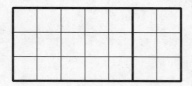

$$7 \times 3$$

$$(5 \times 3) + (2 \times 3)$$

Section B Practice Problems

1. There are 35 books on the bookcase. There are 7 books on each shelf. How many shelves are there? Explain how the equations $35 \div 7 = ?$ and $? \times 7 = 35$ both represent the situation.

_____

_____

_____

_____

(From Unit 4, Lesson 6.)

2. There are 24 eggs in the container. There are 6 in each row. How many rows of eggs are there?

   Write an equation that represents the situation. Use a symbol for the unknown. Then, answer the question.

(From Unit 4, Lesson 7.)

3. For each multiplication equation, write a related division fact you know from the multiplication equation.

   a. $8 \times 5 = 40$

   b. $2 \times 9 = 18$

(From Unit 4, Lesson 8.)

4. Lin knows $8 \times 5 = 40$. Explain how she can use this fact to find 8×4.

_____

_____

(From Unit 4, Lesson 9.)

5.   a. Highlight parts of the diagram to show the expression $(5 \times 7) + (2 \times 7)$.

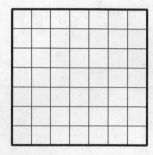

b. Explain how you could use the diagram to calculate 7×7.

_____

_____

(From Unit 4, Lesson 10.)

iM KH

6. Mark or shade the rectangle to show a strategy for finding its area. Then, explain how to use the diagram to find the area.

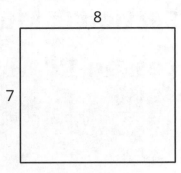

_____

_____

(From Unit 4, Lesson 11.)

7. **Exploration**

Noah finds 9×8 by calculating $(10 \times 8) - (1 \times 8)$.

a. Make a drawing showing why Noah's calculation works.

b. Use Noah's method to calculate 9×8.

Section C: Multiplying Larger Numbers

Lesson 12: Multiply Multiples of Ten

- Let's multiply one-digit numbers times multiples of 10.

Warm-up: Notice and Wonder: Tens

What do you notice? What do you wonder?

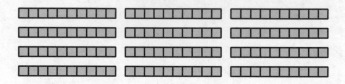

iM KH

12.1: A Whole Lot of Dollars

Six friends are playing a board game that uses play money. The paper bills come in $5, $10, $20, $50, and $100.

1. Every player received $100 to start. Which of the following could be the bills that a player received?

   Write an expression to represent the play bills and the amount in dollars.

bills	expression	dollar amount
one $100 bill		
four $20 bills		
ten $10 bills		
ten $5 bills		
five $20 bills		
twenty $10 bills		
twenty $5 bills		
two $50 bills		

2. At one point in the game, Noah had to pay Lin $150. He gave her that amount using the same type of bill.

   a. Which bill and how many of it could Noah have used to make $150? Name all the possibilities.

   b. Write an expression for each way that Noah could have paid Lin.

3. The table shows what the players had at the end of the game. The person with the most money wins. Who won the game?

Write an expression to represent the bills each person has and the amount in dollars.

player	bills	expression	dollar amount
Andre	nine $10 bills and ten $5 bills		
Clare	fourteen $10 bills		
Jada	ten $10 bills and three $50 bills		
Lin	eight $20 bills		
Noah	six $50 bills		
Tyler	twenty-one $10 bills		

12.2: Two Strategies

1. Two students used base-ten blocks to find the value of 8×30.

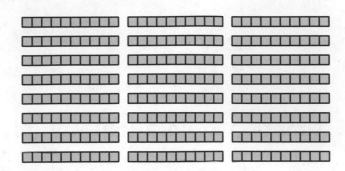

- Jada counted: 30, 60, 90, 120, 150, 180, 210, 240, and said the answer is 240.

- Kiran said he knew 8×3 is 24, then found 24×10 to get 240.

How are Jada and Kiran's strategies alike? How are they different?

2. Find the value of each expression. Explain or show your reasoning.

a. 5×60

b. 8×50

c. 4×30

d. 7×40

e. 9×20

Lesson 13: Solve Problems With Equal Groups

- Let's multiply some teen numbers.

Warm-up: Estimation Exploration: Multiply Teens

$$4 \times 18$$

Record an estimate that is:

too low	about right	too high

iM KH

13.1: Problems with Teen Numbers

Solve each problem. Show your thinking using objects, a drawing, or a diagram.

1. A seller at a farmers market has 7 dozen eggs when they close for the day. How many eggs does the seller have?

2. At the farmers market there's a space for performers to play music with some chairs for people to sit and listen. There are 5 rows of chairs and each row has 15 chairs. How many chairs are there?

3. A booth at a farmers market has a table top that has lengths of 4 feet and 16 feet. What is the area of the table top?

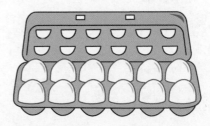

13.2: Gallery Walk: Problems with Teen Numbers

As you visit the posters with your partner, discuss what is the same and what is different about the thinking shown on each poster.

Lesson 14: Ways to Represent Multiplication of Teen Numbers

• Let's make sense of some ways to represent the multiplication of teen numbers.

Warm-up: Notice and Wonder: Seeing Groups

What do you notice? What do you wonder?

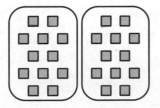 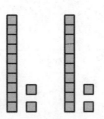 

14.1: A Factor Greater than Ten

1. Tyler says he can use base-ten blocks to find the value of 7×13 because he knows 7×10 and 7×3. He says this diagram proves his thinking.

   Do you agree or disagree? Explain your reasoning.

   _____

   _____

   _____

   _____

2. Use Tyler's method to find the value of 3×14. Explain or show your reasoning.

iM KH

14.2: Ways to Represent

Andre, Clare, and Diego represented the same expression. Their representations are shown below.

Andre

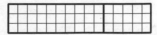

Clare

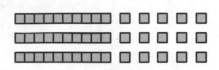

Diego

	10	5
3	30	15

1. Where do you see the factors in each diagram?

2. Where do you see the product in each diagram?

Lesson 15: Equal Groups, Larger Numbers

• Let's solve some problems with equal groups that have larger numbers.

Warm-up: Which One Doesn't Belong: Rectangles

Which one doesn't belong?

A

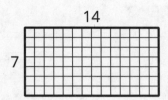
14
7

B

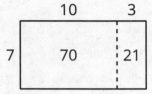
10   3
7   70   21

C

10   4
7   70   28

D

14
7

iM KH

15.1: Equal Groups, Larger Numbers

Solve each problem. Explain or show your reasoning.

1. Noah sees a large painted mural that has side lengths of 15 feet and 4 feet. What is the area of the mural?

2. Noah's family buys a mosaic that has 12 rows and 8 columns of 1 inch tiles. What is the area of the mosaic?

3. At the art festival, Noah uses sidewalk chalk to help decorate a rectangular piece of sidewalk that is 6 feet by 14 feet. What is the area of the piece of sidewalk that Noah helped decorate?

4. At the art festival, Noah buys a pack of stickers. There are 5 sheets and each sheet has 16 stickers. How many stickers are in the pack?

15.2: Gallery Walk: Equal Groups, Larger Numbers

As you visit the posters with your partner, discuss what is the same and what is different about the thinking shown on each poster.

Lesson 16: Multiply Numbers Larger than 20

- Let's multiply numbers that are larger than 20.

Warm-up: Number Talk: Three Times Some Numbers

Find the value of each expression mentally.

- 3×10

- 3×20

- 3×50

- 3×25

16.1: 4×23, Represented

1. Here is how Clare and Andre represented 4×23.

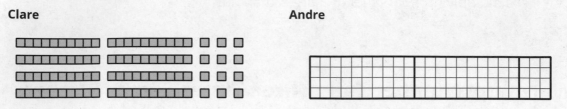

Clare   **Andre**

a. How does each diagram show 4×23?

b. How could we use Clare's diagram to find the value of 4×23?

c. How could we use Andre's diagram to find the value of 4×23?

iM KH

2. Diego tried different ways to partition or split a diagram to help him find the value of 4×23.

A

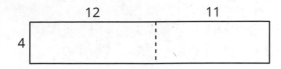

B

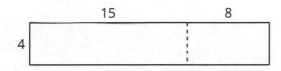

C

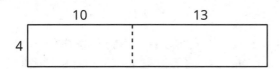

D

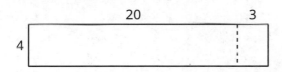

a. What do you notice about the numbers in his diagrams?

b. Which diagram would you use to find the value of 4×23? Explain your reasoning.

3. Find the value of 3×28. Show your thinking using diagrams, symbols, or other representations.

16.2: Some Fine Products

1. To find the value of 2×37, Mai started by writing this equation:

$$2 \times 30 = 60$$

Describe or show what Mai would do to finish finding the value of 2×37.

2. Find the value of each product. Show your reasoning.

   a. 3×32

   b. 2×43

   c. 4×22

   d. 3×29

iM KH

16.3: Play Close to 100, Multiplication

Play Close to 100, Multiplication with a partner.

    1. Place the cards face down.

    2. Each player draws 4 cards.

    3. Each player chooses 2 cards to complete the expression to make a value as close to 100 as possible. Write the 2 digits and the product.

    4. Player closest to 100 wins.

    5. Play 5 rounds. Player who wins the most rounds wins.

Game 1

Round 1

$\boxed{} \times 1\boxed{} = \underline{}$

Round 2

$\boxed{} \times 1\boxed{} = \underline{}$

Round 3

$\boxed{} \times 1\boxed{} = \underline{}$

Round 4

$\boxed{} \times 1\boxed{} = \underline{}$

Round 5

$\boxed{} \times 1\boxed{} = \underline{}$

Game 2

Round 1

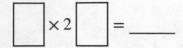

Round 2

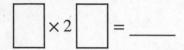

Round 3

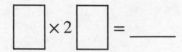

Round 4

$\boxed{} \times 2 \boxed{} = \underline{}$

Round 5

$\boxed{} \times 2 \boxed{} = \underline{}$

Lesson 17: Use the Four Operations to Solve Problems

- Let's use the four operations to solve problems.

Warm-up: True or False: Multiply by 10

Decide if each statement is true or false. Be prepared to explain your reasoning.

- $2 \times 40 = 2 \times 4 \times 10$

- $2 \times 40 = 8 \times 10$

- $3 \times 50 = 15 \times 10$

- $3 \times 40 = 7 \times 10$

17.1: Questions about a Situation

What questions could you ask about this situation?

There are 142 guests at a party. All the guests are in 2 rooms. Room A has 94 guests. Room B has 6 tables that each have the same number of guests. There are 4 pieces of silverware and 1 plate for each guest.

_____

_____

_____

_____

iM KH

17.2: Party Problems

For each problem:

a. Write an equation to represent the situation. Use a letter for the unknown quantity.

b. Solve the problem. Explain or show your reasoning.

1. Kiran is making paper rings each day to decorate for a party. From Monday to Thursday he was able to complete 156 rings. Friday, Kiran and 2 friends worked on making more rings. Each of them made 9 more rings. How many rings did they make over the week?

2. Mai has 168 muffins. She put 104 of the muffins in a basket. She packed the rest of the muffins into 8 boxes with the same number of muffins. How many muffins were in each box?

3. There are 184 cups on a table. Three tables with 8 people at each table come up to get drinks and each use a cup. How many cups are on the table now?

Section C Summary

In this section, we learned how to multiply single-digit numbers by multiples of ten. We used strategies to multiply teen numbers and numbers greater than 20.

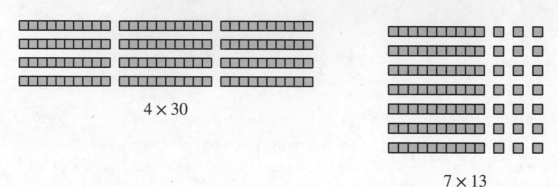

4×30

7×13

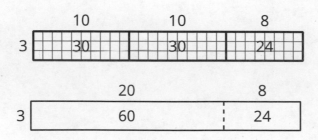

3×28

iM KH

Section C Practice Problems

1. a. How many tens are there in 50?

   b. How many tens are there in 7×50? Explain your reasoning.

   _____

   _____

   c. What is the value of 7×50? Explain your reasoning.

   _____

   _____

   (From Unit 4, Lesson 12.)

2. There are 4 lunch tables. There are 12 students at each table. How many students are there at the tables? Show your thinking using objects, a drawing, or a diagram.

   (From Unit 4, Lesson 13.)

3. a. What do the 60 and 24 in the diagram represent?

_____

_____

b. Explain how to use the diagram to calculate 14 × 6.

_____

_____

(From Unit 4, Lesson 14.)

4. There were 14 days of school in the month. There were 7 hours of school each day. How many hours of school were there during the month?

(From Unit 4, Lesson 15.)

5. Find the value of each expression. Explain or show your reasoning.

a. 2 × 47

b. 3 × 25

(From Unit 4, Lesson 16.)

iM KH

6. A rope is 640 inches long. Andre cuts off 5 pieces of rope that are 16 inches each. How much rope is left?

(From Unit 4, Lesson 17.)

7. **Exploration**

Here is Mai's strategy for calculating 4×21: "First I double 21 and that's 42. Then I double 42 and that's 84."

a. Explain why Mai's strategy works.

_____

_____

b. Use Mai's strategy to find 4×23.

8. **Exploration**

×	1	2	3	4	5	6	7	8	9
1	1	2	3	4	5	6	7	8	9
2	2	4	6	8	10	12	14	16	18
3	3	6	9	12	15	18	21	24	27
4	4	8	12	16	20	24	28	32	36
5	5	10	15	20	25	30	35	40	45
6	6	12	18	24	30	36	42	48	54
7	7	14	21	28	35	42	49	56	63
8	8	16	24	32	40	48	56	64	72
9	9	18	27	36	45	54	63	72	81

a. Make a list of the numbers less than 20 that do not appear in the multiplication table.

b. What do these numbers have in common?

c. Choose one of these numbers and count out that number of objects. Can you make an array out of the objects?

iM KH

9. **Exploration**

Look at the two different diagrams of the same multiplication expression:

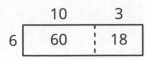 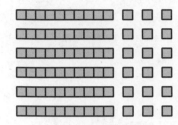

a. What multiplication expression do the two diagrams represent?

b. Can you show a third way to represent the same multiplication expression?

c. What is the value of the expression?

d. Write a story problem to match the expression.

_____

_____

_____

_____

Section D: Dividing Larger Numbers

Lesson 18: Larger Numbers in Equal Groups

- Let's divide with larger numbers.

Warm-up: What Do You Know About Division?

What do you know about division?

18.1: Groups on a Field Trip

There are 48 students going on a field trip to the aquarium. They visit the exhibits in groups of 4 students. How many groups will there be?

Show your thinking using diagrams, symbols, or other representations.

18.2: Bus Ride and Lunch Groups

For each question, show your thinking using diagrams, symbols, or other representations.

1. On another field trip, 72 students and teachers rode in 3 buses to a science museum, with the same number of people in each bus. How many people rode in each bus?

2. During lunch, the 72 people sat at long tables, with 12 people at each table. How many tables did they use?

Lesson 19: Ways to Divide Larger Numbers

- Let's make sense of representations of division.

Warm-up: True or False: Ones, Tens, Twenties

Decide if each statement is true or false. Be prepared to explain your reasoning.

- $4 \times 10 = 40 \times 1$

- $4 \times 20 = 4 \times 2 \times 10$

- $8 \times 20 = 8 \times 2 \times 1$

- $8 \times 20 = 16 \times 10$

19.1: Divide with Base-Ten Blocks

1. Use base-ten blocks to represent each expression. Then, find its value.

    a. $55 \div 5$

    b. $45 \div 3$

2. Find the value of each expression. Use base-ten blocks if you find them helpful.

    a. $63 \div 3$

    b. $84 \div 7$

    c. $100 \div 5$

iM KH

19.2: Different Ways to Show Division

Jada and Han used base-ten blocks to represent $60 \div 5$.

Here is Jada's work:

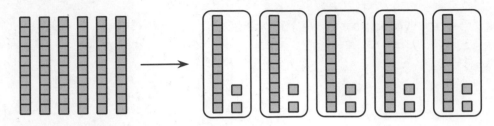

Here's Han's work:

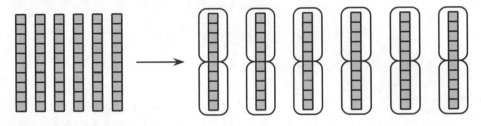

1. Make sense of Jada's and Han's work.

   a. What did they do differently?

   b. Where do we see the value of $60 \div 5$ in each person's work?

2. How would you use base-ten blocks so you could represent these expressions and find their value? Be prepared to explain your reasoning.

   a. $64 \div 4$: Would you make 4 groups or groups of 4?

b. 72 ÷ 6: Would you make 6 groups or groups of 6?

c. 75 ÷ 15: Would you make 15 groups or groups of 15?

Lesson 20: Strategies for Dividing

- Let's use different strategies to divide.

Warm-up: Number Talk: Multiplication and Division

Find the value of each expression mentally.

- 3×5

- 6×5

- 10×5

- $65 \div 5$

20.1: Ways to Divide

1. Lin, Priya, and Tyler found the value of $78 \div 3$. Their work is shown. Make sense of each student's work.

Lin

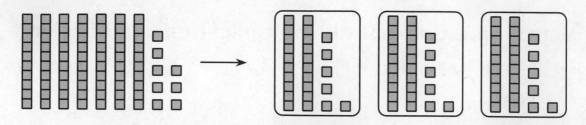

Priya

$3 \times 10 = 30$
$3 \times 10 = 30$
$3 \times 6 = 18$
—————————
$3 \times 26 = 78$

Tyler

$3 \times 20 = 60$
$3 \times 6 = 18$

$20 + 6 = 26$

2. How are the three students' work alike?

3. How are they different?

iM KH

20.2: How Would You Divide?

Find the value of each quotient. Explain or show your reasoning. Organize it so it can be followed by others.

1. $80 \div 5$

2. $68 \div 4$

3. $91 \div 7$

If you have time: Eighty-four students on a field trip are put into groups. Each group has 14 students. How many groups are there?

20.3: Compare, Divide within 100

Play Compare with 2 players.

1. Shuffle the cards and split the deck between the players.

2. Each player turns over a card.

3. Compare the values. The player with the greater value keeps both cards.

4. Play until you run out of cards. The player with the most cards at the end of the game wins.

Lesson 21: Solve Problems Using the Four Operations

- Let's represent and solve problems using all four operations.

Warm-up: Notice and Wonder: Apples Again

What do you notice? What do you wonder?

A farmer picked some apples.
Some of the apples are packed into boxes and some are not.

21.1: Apple Adventure

A farmer picked some apples. Some of the apples are packed into boxes and some are not.

From the list, choose 4 numbers that would make sense together in this situation. Write your choices in the table. Be ready to explain how your numbers make sense together.

400	300	240	12
350	290	230	10
340	280	170	5

total number of apples	number of apples not in boxes	number of boxes	number of apples in each box

iM KH

21.2: Apple Days

Tyler and Clare are helping with a festival at an apple orchard.

1. Tyler is stacking apples to sell at the event. There are 85 apples for his display. He has already made 5 rows of 10 apples. How many apples are left?

   a. Write an equation with a letter for the unknown quantity to represent this situation.

   b. Solve the problem. Explain or show your reasoning.

2. Clare is helping sell baked goods at the event. A customer buys 8 brownies that cost $3 each. Clare adds that money to the cash box and now there is $125 in the cash box. How much money was in the cash box before that purchase?

   a. Write an equation with a letter for the unknown quantity to represent this situation.

   b. Solve the problem. Explain or show your reasoning.

3. The market at the orchard had 200 jars of applesauce for sale. At the end of the event, 184 jars had been sold. The rest of the jars were shared equally among 4 people who work there. How many jars of applesauce did each person get?

    a. Write an equation with a letter for the unknown quantity to represent this situation.

    b. Solve the problem. Explain or show your reasoning.

Section D Summary

In this section, we divided larger numbers and solved problems that involve division.

We used base-ten blocks, diagrams, and equations to represent the numbers we divided. To help us divide, we used what we know about place value, equal groups, and the relationship between multiplication and division.

For example, here are some ways we could find the value of $52 \div 4$:

- Put 5 tens and 2 ones into 4 equal groups.

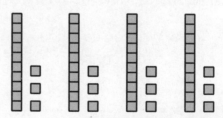

- Think about how many groups of 4 are in 52.

    10 groups of 4 make 40.
    3 groups of 4 make 12.
    13 groups of 4 make 52.

- Use multiplication facts and write equations.

$$4 \times 10 = 40$$
$$4 \times 3 = 12$$

$$10 + 3 = 13$$
$$4 \times 13 = 52$$

At the end of the section, we used all four operations to solve problems.

iM KH

Lesson 22: School Community Garden

- Let's plan a school garden.

Warm-up: Notice and Wonder: Garden

What do you notice? What do you wonder?

22.1: Produce

For each situation, draw a diagram and write an equation or expression.

1. A strawberry patch has 7 rows with 8 strawberry plants in each row.

   a. How many strawberry plants are in the patch?

   b. To grow strawberries in the best way, the rows should be 4 feet apart. Each plant in the row should be 2 feet apart. How long and wide is the strawberry patch?

   c. You can harvest 12 strawberries per plant. How many strawberries will grow in each row?

2. With your partner, take turns explaining where you see the numbers in the expression or equation you wrote in your diagram.

22.2: Plan the Garden

1. Read the information about some plants you could grow in a garden. Then, circle 2 plants to grow in your part of the school garden.

    a. strawberries

    b. cantaloupe

    c. zucchini

    d. tomatoes

    e. pinto beans

    f. potatoes

2. Plan your garden. Both of your plants should harvest between 50–100 fruits or vegetables.

    a. How many of each plant will you grow?

    b. Predict how many fruits or vegetables you will harvest. Show or explain your reasoning.

3. Make a diagram that shows how the plants are arranged and how much space is needed.

Growing Requirements

strawberries

- Grow in patches
- Space rows: 4 feet apart
- Space plants: 2 feet apart
- Each plant produces 12 strawberries.

cantaloupes

- Grow on vines
- Space rows: 4 feet apart
- Space plants: 1 foot apart
- Each plant produces about 8 cantaloupes.

zucchini

- Grow on vines
- Space rows: 5 feet apart
- Space plants: 1 foot apart
- Each plant produces about 8 zucchini.

tomatoes

- Grow on vines
- Space rows: 4 feet apart
- Space plants: 2 feet apart
- Each plant produces about 20 tomatoes.

pinto beans

- Grow on bushes in pods
- Space rows: 2 feet apart
- Space plants: 1 foot apart
- Each plant produces 20–25 pods and each pod produces about 5 beans.

potatoes

- Grow in rows
- Space rows: 2–3 feet apart
- Space plants: 1 foot apart
- Each plant produces 5–10 potatoes.

Section D Practice Problems

1. There are 85 chairs in the gym. They are arranged in 5 rows with the same number of chairs in each row. How many chairs are in each row? Show your thinking using diagrams, symbols, or other representations.

(From Unit 4, Lesson 18.)

2.   a. Find the value of $96 \div 6$. Use base-ten blocks if they are helpful.

b. Find the value of $52 \div 4$. Use base-ten blocks if they are helpful.

(From Unit 4, Lesson 19.)

3.   a. Find the value of $78 \div 6$. Draw a diagram if it is helpful.

b. Find the value of $42 \div 3$. Draw a diagram if it is helpful.

(From Unit 4, Lesson 20.)

4. Find the value of each quotient.

    a. $96 \div 6$

    b. $87 \div 3$

(From Unit 4, Lesson 20.)

5. There are 240 people at the park for the soccer games. There are 150 fans. The rest of the people are on 6 soccer teams with an equal number of players. How many players are on each soccer team?

    a. Write an equation to represent this situation. Use a letter for the unknown quantity.

    b. Solve the problem. Explain or show your reasoning.

(From Unit 4, Lesson 21.)

iM KH

6. **Exploration**

To find the value of $96 \div 3$, Diego divides 9 by 3 and 6 by 3 and says the answer is 32.

a. Explain why Diego's method is correct. Use equations or drawings to support your reasoning.

b. Does Diego's method work to find the value of $78 \div 3$? Explain your reasoning.

_____

_____

_____

_____

7. **Exploration**

What are the different ways you can divide 48 objects into equal groups?

a. Make a list.

b. Write a multiplication or division equation for each different way.

Glossary

algorithm

A set of steps that works every time as long as the steps are carried out correctly.

area

The number of square units that cover a flat figure without gaps or overlaps.

array

An arrangement of objects in rows and columns. Each column must contain the same number of objects as the other columns, and each row must have the same number of objects as the other rows.

bar graph

A way to show how many in each group or category using the length of rectangles.

division

Finding the number of groups or finding the size of each group when we share into groups of equal size.

divisor

The number we are dividing by which can represent the size of the groups or the number of groups.

equation

A statement that includes an equal sign (=). It tells us that what is on one side of the sign is equal to what is on the other side.

expanded form

A specific way of writing a number as a sum of hundreds, tens, and ones.

Expanded form writes a number as a sum of the value of each digit. Example: 482 written in expanded form is $400 + 80 + 2$.

expression

An expression has at least 2 numbers and at least one math operation (such as addition, subtraction, multiplication and division).

factor

When we multiply two whole numbers to get a product, each of those numbers is a factor of the product.

key
The part of a picture graph that tells what each picture represents.

multiplication
The operation that tells you the total number of objects when you have a certain number of equal groups.

parentheses
Grouping symbols that can be used in expressions or equations, such as:
$(3 \times 5) + (2 \times 5), (24 \div 2) + 5 = 17$.

picture graph
A way to show how many in each group or category using pictures of the objects or symbols.

product
The result of multiplying some numbers.

quotient
The result in a division equation.

rounding
A formal way to say which number a given number is closer to. For example, for 182, the number 180 is the closest multiple of ten and 200 is the closest multiple of a hundred. We can round 182 to 180 (if rounding to the nearest ten) or 200 (if rounding to the nearest hundred).

scaled bar graph
A bar graph marked in multiples of some number other than 1.

scaled picture graph
A picture graph where each picture represents an amount other than 1.

square centimeter
A square with side lengths of 1 centimeter.

square foot
A square with side lengths of 1 foot.

square inch
A square with side lengths of 1 inch.

square meter
A square with side lengths of 1 meter.

Attributions

The Common Core State Standards are trademarks of the Common Core State Standards Initiative. © Copyright 2010. National Governors Association Center for Best Practices and Council of Chief State School Officers. All rights reserved. http://www.corestandards.org/

"Notice and Wonder" and "I Notice/I Wonder" are trademarks of the National Council of Teachers of Mathematics, reflecting approaches developed by the Math Forum (http://www.nctm.org/noticeandwonder/), and used here with permission.

Images that are not the original work of Illustrative Mathematics are in the public domain or released under a Creative Commons Attribution (CC-BY) license, and include an appropriate citation. Images that are the original work of Illustrative Mathematics do not include such a citation.

Image Attributions

By José Joey. Pixabay. Pixabay. https://pixabay.com/photos/waterfall-igua%C3%A7u-nature-cataracts-5040210/.

Washington Monument in Washington DC, by Alvesgaspar . CC BY-SA 4.0. Wikimedia Commons. https://en.wikipedia.org/wiki/Washington_Monument#/media/File:Washington_October_2016-6_(cropped)_(cropped).jpg.

Lincoln Memorial, east side, by Martin Falbisoner. CC-BY-SA 3.0. Wikimedia. https://commons.wikimedia.org/wiki/File:Lincoln_Memorial_east_side.JPG#/media/File:Lincoln_Memorial_east_side.JPG.

Tour Eiffel, by Benh Lieu Song. CC BY 3.0. Wikimedia Commons. https://commons.wikimedia.org/wiki/File:Tour_Eiffel_Wikimedia_Commons.jpg.

SDMB Drill Formation of a Pitchfork during Pregame 2007, by Jason Crews. CC BY 2.0. Wikipedia. https://en.wikipedia.org/wiki/Sun_Devil_Marching_Band#/media/File:SDMB_Pitchfork_Drill_Formation.jpg.

By Gaby Stein. Pixabay. Pixabay. https://pixabay.com/photos/wood-beads-colorful-color-wood-262075/.

By Evan Ellis. Pexel License. Pexels. https://www.pexels.com/photo/wood-people-technology-music-4015926/.

By Pavel Bokr. Pixabay. Pixabay. https://pixabay.com/photos/apples-fruit-apple-fetus-1642732/.

By Petr Kratochvil. CC0. PublicDomainPictures.net. https://www.publicdomainpictures.net/en/view-image.php?image=267667&picture=apple-orchard.

By Alberto Adán. Pixabay. Pixabay. https://pixabay.com/photos/wooden-spinning-top-top-mexican-3868460/.

By PublicDomainPictures. Pixabay. Pixabay. https://pixabay.com/photos/dreidels-hanukkah-spinning-tops-20347/.

By CalculaPR. Pixabay. Pixabay. https://pixabay.com/photos/whirligig-traditional-folklore-wood-2316859/.

Spinning Top, by Federlight. CC BY-SA 4.0. Wikimedia Commons. https://commons.wikimedia.org/wiki/File:Spinning_Top.jpeg.

By Anthony. Pexel License. Pexels. https://www.pexels.com/photo/blue-and-green-spin-toy-170288/.

By Nicholas Caffarilla. CC-BY-SA 3.0. Wikipedia. https://en.wikipedia.org/wiki/Insect#/media/File:Insect_collage.png.

By Martin Winkler. Pixabay. Pixabay. https://pixabay.com/photos/market-vegetable-market-1558658/.

By Capri23auto. Pixabay. Pixabay. https://pixabay.com/photos/apple-apple-tree-fruit-3535566/.

By Silvia Thor. Pixabay. Pixabay. https://pixabay.com/photos/garden-strawberries-plant-red-934189/.

By Fruchthandel_Magazin. Pixabay. Pixabay. https://pixabay.com/photos/strawberries-red-sweet-plant-field-196798/.

By Davgood Kirshot. Pixabay. Pixabay. https://pixabay.com/photos/cantaloupe-fruit-melon-healthy-3634128/.

By Monika. Pixabay. Pixabay. https://pixabay.com/photos/zucchini-vegetables-cultivation-1522535/.

By kie-ker. Pixabay. Pixabay. https://pixabay.com/photos/tomatoes-vines-water-droplets-wet-1561565/.

Pinto beans, main crop at Pie Town, New Mexico, by Russell Lee. Public Domain. Wikimedia Commons. https://commons.wikimedia.org/wiki/File:Pinto_beans,_main_crop_1a34133v.jpg.

By IlonaF. Pixabay. Pixabay. https://pixabay.com/photos/potatoes-tubers-arable-agriculture-3690562/.

Citations

Unit 3: Wrapping Up Addition and Subtraction Within 1,000

Lesson 2

Iguazu Falls. *Wikipedia, The Free Encyclopedia*. Retrieved from https://en.wikipedia.org/wiki/Iguazu_Falls

Lesson 2

Lincoln Memorial. *Wikipedia, The Free Encyclopedia*. Retrieved from https://en.wikipedia.org/wiki/Lincoln_Memorial

Lesson 2

Toureiffel.Paris. *The Official Website of the Eiffel Tower*. Retrieved from https://www.toureiffel.paris/en/faq/spot/how-can-you-climb-eiffel-tower-foot

Lesson 2

Washington Monument. *Wikipedia, The Free Encyclopedia*. Retrieved from https://en.wikipedia.org/wiki/Washington_Monument

Notes

Notes

Notes

Notes

Notes

Notes